GW00630565

THE EXPERIENCE & GROWTH IN LIFE

Witness Lee

Living Stream Ministry

Anaheim, CA • www.lsm.org

© 1989 Living Stream Ministry

First Edition, April 1990.

ISBN 978-0-87083-508-7

Published by

Living Stream Ministry
2431 W. La Palma Ave., Anaheim, CA 92801 U.S.A.
P. O. Box 2121, Anaheim, CA 92814 U.S.A.

Printed in the United States of America
10   11   12   13   14   15   /   12   11   10   9   8   7   6

CONTENTS

PREFACE

This book is composed of messages given by Brother Witness Lee in the full-time training in Anaheim, California in the fall of 1989.

THE EXPERIENCE AND GROWTH IN LIFE

MESSAGE ONE

THE EXPERIENCE OF LIFE

(1)

This series of messages was given by Brother Witness Lee in the full-time training in Anaheim in the fall of 1989.

Scripture Reading: Eph. 4:18; Rom. 8:2; John 10:10; 6:35, 55, 57; 6:63; Gen. 1:26-27; 2:7; Rev. 2:7; 22:2

Prayer: Lord, we thank You for Your sovereignty, and we thank You for Your sovereign grace that we may have this training. Lord, we believe it is of You, yet we still put our trust in You. We have no trust in ourselves. We trust in You for all the trainees. Grant them Your merciful, gracious visitation every day. Lord, this morning we look unto You for Your speaking. Speak a word out of Your heart to our heart. We need Your word of life. Reveal life to us. Lord, do cover us, fight the battle, and condemn the evil one. We ask You, and we even give You the command, to defeat him in these fighting days. Lord, defeat the enemy. We bind him. O Lord, thank You. Give us a living word. Amen.

AN INTRODUCTORY WORD
CONCERNING THE TRAINING

This is a very special and particular training. We have never had such a training as this in the past sixty years. First, I will not speak very much. I will only speak four times each week out of the eighteen to nineteen classes. I will speak Tuesday morning, Thursday morning, Saturday morning, and one evening. I hope this will encourage you rather than disappoint you.

Second, there will be ten other teachers to help you. They are willing to participate in this training for a period of sixteen weeks. Most of them will speak once or twice a week, while a few of them will speak as many as three times a week. So, including myself, you will have eleven brothers helping you.

Third, the visiting work which will be assigned to you beginning tonight will consist of four things: to visit people as the priests of the New Testament gospel, to feed and nourish the newly saved ones in the home meetings, to endeavor to build up small groups in order to perfect the new ones, and to raise up new churches in new cities. We have never had such a long-term training with such special daily practices.

In the visiting work, especially concerning the small groups, there is much to learn. Many of the so-called small groups which have been meeting for some time are too natural. For the most part they are not according to the way of the New Testament economy. Rather, they are according to the natural understanding. Some may say that they know what a small group is and that all that is needed is to group people together. I would say a strong no to this. The small group is the practice of perfecting the saints revealed in Ephesians 4:12; hence, it is a great thing. The small group is not only for your perfecting, but also for you to perfect others. However, before you can perfect others, you yourself must learn. This is why we will spend a lot of energy in this training to strengthen your learning.

In raising up new churches, we will assign some of you to new, nearby cities. You will be formed into teams of three persons each. Two new teams, six persons, will be sent to take care of a new city. Within the sixteen weeks of the training, I hope that a number of new, small churches will be raised up in those new cities. After the sixteen weeks of training are completed, when you go, another group of new trainees will come to continue the work. This is a particular aspect of the visiting work in this training.

THE CONTENT OF THE TRAINING—THE GROWTH IN LIFE AND THE PRACTICE OF THE NEW WAY

In this term of training, I do not have the burden to release any new vision as I have done in special meetings and conferences in the past. I will just sit down to converse with you concerning two main things: the growth in life and the practice of the new way. According to spiritual sequence, life should be first and the new way second, but according to my burden, the new way should be first. I will spend sixteen hours, one hour each week, to talk to you about the new way. The new way has been misunderstood, rejected, and even, to some extent, slandered. Some have said that the full-time training in Taipei was a "Hagar" and that all the ones baptized through door-knocking were "Ishmaels." This is a very serious, evil slander. So I must spend some time to give sixteen talks about the new way.

I will speak four times each week concerning these two things, dealing with them in different ways. Related to the matter of life, what I will talk with you about is the experience of life and the growth in life. Concerning the new way, we will spend some time to look into the new way, and we will also talk about the exercise of the new way. Even though I have released quite a number of messages in the past four and a half years about the new way, there is still the need of some deeper insight concerning the new way.

ONLY THE ETERNAL LIFE OF GOD IS LIFE

Perhaps most of you have read the book entitled *The Experience of Life*. The messages contained in that book were given in 1953 and 1954 and printed two or three years later. So this book has been among us for many years. However, today, though I may refer to that book, I will not speak according to that book. Rather, I will talk to you according to your situation.

What is life? Or who is life? According to the Scriptures, in the whole universe, there is only one life. All the other lives may be considered "non-life" because they are temporal lives. There are many different kinds of life, such as that of the mosquitos, termites, ants, wolves, dogs, and tigers. There are also different categories of life, such as the vegetable life and the animal life. The highest of all these created lives is the human life. Yet, all of these lives, including the human life, are temporal.

Only one life exists without beginning and without ending. Only one life is the source of life, the substance of life, the element of life, and the factor of life. This life is called the eternal life. This life is eternal, not only in time, but also in source, in substance, in element, and in factor. Eternal means unlimited and unrestricted. This eternal life is not bound, limited, or restricted in time, in source, in substance, in element, or in factor. In every aspect and in every regard, this life is unlimited and unrestricted. This life is eternal in every way. The Bible tells us that when we believed into the Lord Jesus, we received such an eternal life (John 3:16).

Many Christians do not understand the term *eternal life.* Have you ever heard that this eternal life is eternal not only in time but also in quality, substance, element, factor, and even in its source? With all the other lives, the created lives, there are some restrictions. For instance, we have strength, but our strength is limited. We have might, power, and ability, but we are limited in each one of these things. We are very limited in our might, our power, and our strength. We as human beings have more strength, power, and ability than any other created life; yet our strength, power, and ability are all with some restriction and limitation. We may be able to endure, but regardless how long we can endure, our endurance is limited. God's endurance, however, is not limited. Only one life, the eternal life, is unlimited in every way. This eternal life is not only of God but is the very God Himself.

GOD, CHRIST, THE SPIRIT, AND THE WORD BEING LIFE

In the entire New Testament, the term *the life of God* is only mentioned once, in Ephesians 4:18. The term *the life of God* indicates that God is life just as the phrases *the love of God* (1 John 4:9; 2 Cor. 13:14) and *the light of the Lord* (Isa. 2:5) indicate that God is love (1 John 4:8, 16) and God is light (1 John 1:5), respectively. These phrases are synonyms. All are in the form of appositions. In the phrase *the life of God, life* and *God* are also in apposition. God is life, God is love, and God is light.

The eternal life, the divine life, is the very God of whom is life, and who is the Spirit. Life is God Himself, God is Spirit (John 4:24), and the Spirit is life (Rom. 8:2). The eternal life, the divine life, is also the Spirit of life. God the Spirit, has embodied Himself in Christ (John 4:24; 1:1, 14). The life of God, God Himself, is also the life of Christ, Christ Himself. Actually in the New Testament, there is no such term as *the life of Christ*. It simply states that Christ is life (John 14:6; 11:25).

Life is eternal. Life is divine. Life is Christ. Christ is God, and Christ is the Spirit. The eternal, divine life which is God, the Spirit, and Christ is embodied in the word. The New Testament says that the word is life (John 6:63; 1 John 1:1). This life is embodied not only in the words spoken by God but also in His word spoken by us. Acts 5:20 reveals that the word spoken out of Peter's mouth was the word of this life. Peter's speaking was not only the word of God, but the word of his testimony. Peter's life and work made the divine life so real and present in his situation; hence, it was the word of his testimony.

The entire content of the Bible, especially the New Testament, is life. Life is its center. Life is the substance, element, and factor of the entire New Testament. The New Testament is a book of "this life" (Acts 5:20), the eternal life.

MAN WITH GOD'S IMAGE, LIKENESS, AND BREATH

Life being the content of the Bible is fully signified by the tree of life (Gen. 2:9). In order to know the significance of the tree of life, we must consider the background of chapters one and two of the book of Genesis. The book of Genesis portrays the tree of life with a certain kind of background. According to Genesis 1 and 2, God created man as the center of His creatures, the center of His creation. Man was created in God's image, according to God's likeness. Outwardly, in appearance, man bears God's image and has God's likeness (Gen. 1:26-27), and inwardly, God's breath has entered into man (Gen. 2:7). The Hebrew word for breath in Genesis 2:7 is *neshamah*. This word *neshamah* is also used in Proverbs 20:27 and is translated *spirit*. This is a crucial verse, and I encourage you to learn it. Proverbs 20:27 says, "The spirit of man is the lamp of Jehovah" (Heb.). By looking at the usage of the word *neshamah* in these two verses, we can see that when the breath was with God it was a breath (Gen. 2:7). But when this breath entered into man it became man's spirit (Prov. 20:27). By this we can see that the spirit of man is very much linked with God.

Genesis 1 and 2 show us that man is outwardly made in God's image, according to God's likeness, and that inwardly he is filled with God's breath. The breath of God became man's spirit for man to contact God, to receive God, and to contain God. These two portions of Genesis, 1:26-27 and 2:7, show us that man is a vessel. His outward appearance is like God, and his inward parts are linked with God. Although at the time of his creation man had all of these things, he still did not have God within him. Man did not have the life of God within him. Man only had the breath of God, but that breath was neither God Himself nor was it God's life. This breath linked man with God by forming man's spirit.

MAN AS AN EATING VESSEL BEFORE
THE TREE OF LIFE

The picture shown by these portions of the Word is that God created man as an eating vessel. To eat is to receive, digest, and assimilate food. In this way, whatever you eat will eventually become you. Last night I ate a very good fish. Before I ate the fish, it was fish. But this morning while I am sitting here, the fish is becoming me. It was received by me last night at dinner. Later, I digested it. A little later, it was assimilated into me, and eventually this morning it has become me. Look at the picture in Genesis 1 and 2. Man was created as a vessel with God's image and likeness outwardly and with a spirit as a receiver inside. After man was created in this way, God brought him to the tree of life (Gen. 2:9). This tree of life was good for food. This is like bringing someone to a dining table. Once he eats the food, he begins to digest and assimilate the food. Eventually the food becomes part of him.

Before man could eat of the tree of life, the Bible tells us that Satan the Devil, through the serpent, distracted man (Gen. 3:1-6). Thus, man was separated from the tree of life (Gen. 3:22-24). Eventually, the Lord Jesus came that we may have life and have it abundantly (John 10:10). The life the Lord came to bring us is the life of the tree of life, a tree which is good for food (Gen. 2:9). In the Gospel of John, the Lord also told us that He is the vine tree (John 15:1, 5) and that He is food (6:35, 55), good for eating (vv. 51, 53, 57). The picture in these verses in the Gospel of John is the same picture as that in Genesis 2. In Genesis 2 man was placed before the tree of life, and in the Gospel of John we are told to eat Jesus, who is the tree of life (John 15:1).

In Revelation 2:7, after the churches had become degraded, the Lord came in to call the overcomers to eat the tree of life. The overcomers are those who are eating Jesus as the tree of life in the church life today. This eating of the tree of life today signifies that the tree of life will be in the New Jerusalem in the millennium. Today in the church life as overcomers, we are eating Jesus as the tree of life, and tomorrow all the overcomers will be eating Jesus as the tree of life in the New Jerusalem during the thousand year millennial kingdom. Ultimately, in eternity the tree of life will be in the center of the New Jerusalem (Rev. 22:2). The tree of life will feed all of God's redeemed people for eternity.

God is not a religion. God is life and He is for life. Today, this life is in the word (John 6:63). Therefore, we must come to the word and eat it. In the new way we all must learn to prophesy. In order to prophesy we must eat the word. God is life and He is for life, and this life is in the word. So we must come to the word and eat it. We have received this life by eating the word. The way to eat the word is by exercising our spirit to take the word. Our spirit is our organ to receive God. So every day, all the time, we must exercise this organ to take the word. In this way, we receive life. This is the experience of life. The experience of life is just to exercise our spirit to eat the word that we may receive life. After being received by us, this life will live out all kinds of divine, spiritual, and heavenly things in an unlimited way.

THE EXPERIENCE AND GROWTH IN LIFE

MESSAGE TWO

THE GROWTH IN LIFE

(1)

Scripture Reading: Col. 2:19; 1 Cor. 3:6-7, 9; 1 Pet. 2:2

In this series of messages we shall consider the growth in life. Colossians 2:19, 1 Corinthians 3:6-7 and 9, and 1 Peter 2:2 are the best verses in the New Testament related to the growth in life. Ephesians 4:13-16 speaks of the growth of the Body rather than the growth in life of the members individually.

GROWING WITH THE GROWTH OF GOD

First Corinthians 3:6-7 says, "I planted, Apollos watered, but God made to grow; so that neither is the one who plants anything nor the one who waters, but the One who makes to grow, God." Verse 9 says, "For we are God's fellow workers; you are God's farm, God's building." Growth in these verses is not the growth in knowledge because here Paul speaks of a farm. Planting and watering are not related to knowledge. To plant is not to instruct but to nourish by supplying the plant with fertile soil. Likewise, to water is not to teach but to supply the plant with nutrients in the water. This is related to life.

Colossians 2:19 says, "Holding the Head, out from whom all the Body, by means of the joints and bands being supplied and knit together, grows with the growth of God." These verses show us that to grow is to grow with something. If a young boy does not eat or drink, he will have nothing with which to grow. One cannot grow with nothing. Rather, without something with which to grow, one will die. Dietitians tell us that we are what we eat. If we eat beef, we will be constituted with the meat of the cow. If we eat fish, we will be constituted with fish.

God created man in His own image according to His own likeness (Gen. 1:26). Then He breathed His breath into man, and after getting into man, that breath became man's spirit (Gen. 2:7; Zech. 12:1). These are the two particular characteristics of the created man. Outwardly man has God's image, and inwardly man has God's breath as his own spirit. Strictly speaking, however, God's breath alone is not His life. God's life is God Himself, the divine Person. At the time of his creation, man did not have God's life, God Himself, within him. He had only God's image as His expression. This image may be compared to a photograph. My photograph may bear my image, but it does not have me in it. The life within the created man was only man's life, and after the fall this life became death itself.

This created man was made as a vessel (Rom. 9:21-23) with the ability to eat. To eat is to receive, digest, assimilate, and retain something organic. Anything that is not organic is not good for food. Something must be organic for us to eat it, and as we have seen, whatever we eat eventually becomes us. Therefore, we must be careful about our eating. To be careful about eating is the first charge that God gave to man (Gen. 2:16-17). In Genesis 2 God did not give Adam commandments concerning his conduct. The commandments concerning faithfulness, lying, stealing, and obedience to parents were given after the fall. Before the fall, right after God's creation of man, God gave only one charge. Genesis 2:16-17a says, "And the Lord God commanded the man, saying, Of every tree of the garden thou mayest freely eat: but of the tree of the knowledge of good and evil, thou shalt not eat of it." The tree of life was good for food, and the tree of the knowledge of good and evil was also good for food. Even today there are two trees among us. One tree is God as life. If we eat this tree, we become life. The other tree is the source of death, Satan. If we eat him, we receive the source of death, that is, we receive him as death. Romans 8:6 says, "For the mind set on the flesh is death, but the mind set on the spirit is life and peace." If we

eat life, we will receive life and will become life, but if we eat
death, we will not only die but will become death.

GROWING NOT BY TEACHING BUT BY SUPPLY

According to our natural concept, we cannot understand
the growth in life. Today there are not many Christians who
know what the growth in life is. Someone who is accustomed
to losing his temper may one day be able to control his temper. This may or may not be the growth in life. The Bible has
life, and it also has some amount of teaching. Without the
teachings of Christianity for the past twenty centuries, the
Western world might be barbaric. The Western world, from
Europe to America, has received its proper teachings from
Christianity. However, Christianity today has become a religion of teaching. When I was young, I heard an American
pastor say that Christianity is the same as Confucianism.
According to him, Confucius taught that we should honor our
parents, and the Bible says the same thing. Ethically speaking, the Bible does appear to be the same as the teachings of
Confucius, and to some extent it may not even appear to be as
high. The Bible teaches submission, but Confucius taught
threefold submission. He taught that a girl in her father's
house should submit herself to her father; when she marries,
she should submit herself to her husband; and when her husband dies, she must submit herself to her son.

The Bible does not annul the teaching of submission.
Rather, it supports it very much. Without the father, husband,
or son as God's deputy authority, the human race would
become as the beasts. There could be no proper marriage life,
family, or nation—only anarchy. However, the growth in life is
not by teaching but by supply. As we have seen, to plant is not
to teach, and to water is not to instruct. Planting and watering
have nothing to do with knowledge but rather are a matter of
supply.

GROWING BY BEING GRAFTED

As men we were the wild olive tree (Rom. 11:17). How
could we become the cultivated olive tree (v. 24)? To be cultivated does not merely mean to be educated or regulated. It

mainly means to be nourished and fed. The wild olive tree can become cultivated only by being grafted. To carry out the grafting, the first thing needed is cutting. Grafting depends upon cutting both trees, the wild tree and the cultivated tree. The branch of the wild tree must be cut off, and an opening must be cut in the cultivated tree. Then the wild branch is put into the cultivated tree. They touch each other, and the wild branch receives the rich life-juice of the cultivated tree, that is, it eats, absorbs, and receives the riches of the cultivated tree. All the riches of the cultivated tree are digested and assimilated by the grafted branch. The wild branch retains the rich juice, and the rich juice eventually becomes the very grafted branch.

This is a good picture showing us how to grow. First, we must be cut off from the old, wild, uncultivated tree of Adam. This is the meaning of baptism. To be baptized is to be cut off from the Adamic race and to be put into death. This was what John the Baptist did. When some repented, he did not teach them. Rather, he cut them off and put them into death by putting them into the water.

Second, we must believe. To believe is to put the branch which has been cut off into Christ as the cultivated tree full of rich life-juice. After we are put into Him, we then remain in Him (John 15:4). As those who are no longer merely the uncultivated branches but the branches grafted into the cultivated tree, Christ, we should remain there to receive, absorb, assimilate, and retain the rich life-juice of Christ in our being. In this way we will surely grow in life. We will grow with the growth of the tree, which is Christ, the embodiment of God.

According to Colossians 2:19, we, holding the Head, grow with the growth of God. The King James Version translates the last part of this verse as "increaseth with the increase of God." To grow is to increase. At first a tree may have only ten branches. The tree is real, yet it is not increasing. When the other branches from the wild tree are grafted into this cultivated tree, it increases from ten branches to one hundred branches. These one hundred branches are the increase of the tree. In this way all the grafted branches grow with the growth of the cultivated tree. This is the way we grow with the growth of God.

When I first saw the last phrase of Colossians 2:19 translated as "grows with the growth of God," I asked myself whether God grows. God is eternal. How could the eternal God grow or increase? In God Himself there is no need of increase. He is complete, perfect, and eternal. However, God needs to grow in us. When God grows in us, we grow in His growth. If God does not have a way to grow in us, we can never grow.

GROWING BY EXERCISING OUR SPIRIT

The divine life is God, and God is a Spirit. If He were like a piece of gold and not a Spirit, how could He get into us? He must be a Spirit to get into us. Furthermore, God can get into man only because man has something that has come out of God, the breath of God, which became man's spirit. To grow in the growth of life is altogether a matter of the divine Spirit and the human spirit. We, who have the breath of God as our spirit, must grow by this spirit. In order to grow in life we should not merely exercise our mind. We all need bodily exercise, but this does not help us to grow in life either. To grow in God as life we must exercise our spirit. When we exercise our spirit, we make the way for God to grow.

The unbelievers do not have God growing in them because they do not know how to exercise their spirit. For this reason we have to go to them to tell them that they need God. They need to speak something out of the depths of their being, their spirit. If they do this, they will exercise their spirit, and when they exercise their spirit, God will have a way to enter into them. The real salvation is the grafting of an uncultivated, wild branch into Christ as the cultivated tree.

We all have to learn to preach the gospel in this way rather than in the old way. The old way is to say, "Dear friend, you are a sinner. Today you are living a poor life, always sinning and fighting with others. You don't have happiness, and, moreover, you will go to hell. Therefore, you have to repent. Jesus died for you, and you can be forgiven. Then you will have a happy life, and you will go to a happy place, heaven." This is not the deeper gospel. This is the shallow gospel.

When the Lord raised up new light among us, the new way, and brought us into it, a certain number of arguments were aroused. Some said that to preach the gospel was not something new; they had done it before and were still doing it. However, in what way are we preaching the gospel? It may be in the shallow way. Many Christians do not know how to preach the gospel in a deeper way. The deeper gospel is something new, yet something ancient. It is in the Bible but not in man's natural understanding. Therefore, I have the burden to conduct a training. I would like to train the saints to know things, not in a superficial way but in a deep way. When we preach the gospel in this deeper way, we do not touch the "flesh and bone" of man; we touch the spirit of man. Go to preach such a gospel and touch the spirit of man. When man touches his own spirit, God has a way to enter into him. Then this man is grafted into Christ; he is saved.

We must remember the principle of our growth in the divine life. To grow in life is to grow with the growth of life. It is to increase with the increase of God who is life.

THE EXPERIENCE AND GROWTH IN LIFE

MESSAGE THREE

THE EXPERIENCE OF LIFE

(2)

Scripture Reading: John 6:57; 14:19; Gal. 2:20; Phil. 1:21; Rom. 6:4-5; 11:24

THE REVELATION OF LIVING CHRIST
IN THE NEW TESTAMENT

In the New Testament, there are four main verses—two in the Gospels and two in the Epistles—which reveal the matter of living Christ. The first verse, John 6:57, says, "As the living Father sent Me, and I live because of the Father, so he who eats Me shall also live because of Me." This is the first verse in the New Testament that directly touches the matter of living Christ. The second verse is also in the Gospel of John. John 14:19 says, "Yet a little while and the world beholds Me no longer, but you behold Me; because I live, you shall live also." The phrase "because I live" means that Christ lives in resurrection. "Yet a little while" indicates His death and that He will live again in His resurrection. The clause "because I live, you shall live also" indicates that because He lives in resurrection, we also shall live with Him and by Him. In the New Testament, John 6:57 and 14:19 are the most basic verses in unveiling to us how we can live because of Christ and with Christ. The third verse, perhaps the best in the Epistles concerning our living because of Christ and with Christ, is Galatians 2:20. It says, "I have been crucified with Christ, and it is no longer I who live, but Christ lives in me; and the life which I now live in the flesh I live in faith."

The fourth verse is Philippians 1:21 which says, "For to me to live is Christ."

LIVING BECAUSE OF CHRIST

By these four verses, we can learn how to live Christ. In this matter, I do not use the phrase *live by Christ* because the word *by* does not convey the proper thought. In John 6:57 the word "because" implies that there is a factor. The word *by* (used in the KJV), however, indicates an instrument, not a factor. To walk *by* Christ implies that Christ is the instrument for walking, as a cane is used for walking. To walk *because* of Him indicates that He is the factor of our walking. This understanding is also the meaning in the Greek. John 14:19 reveals that we live Christ in His resurrection. After His resurrection He lives, and we live also. We do not merely live by Him but because of Him.

We do not live by Christ, taking Christ as our instrument; rather, we live *because of* Christ, taking Christ as a factor of our living. The food that we eat is not an instrument, but a supplying factor. We live not by food but because of the food. Food supplies us so that we can live because of its supply. In using a cane as an instrument to walk, there is no need to eat the cane; but to live because of food, we must eat the food. Without eating, food cannot become a factor of our living. We live Christ in His resurrection, and we live Christ by eating Him. Eating brings in a factor to our being. When we eat a good breakfast in the morning, the nourishment we receive energizes us. The energizing element of Christ is a supply, a factor, for us to live Christ.

Galatians 2:20 says, "It is no longer I who live, but Christ lives in me." Christ has been eaten by us, and now He is within us, living within us. While He is living within us, He is being digested by us. The way Christ lives in us is by being digested by us. He now has become the supply, the very factor, with which we live. We live with Christ as the supplying factor. The clause "it is no longer I who live" means that we are finished. Yet the later clause "the life which I now live" indicates that we continue to live. In order to describe this experience, we may say, "Christ lives for me." However, it is better to say that Christ lives within us to be the factor for us to live with Him. According to Galatians 2:20, there seems to be two who live. There are two subjects, "Christ" and "I," and these two subjects act on one predicate—live. "I live" and "Christ lives."

In order to describe one living with two lives, Paul used the illustration of grafting (Rom. 11:24; 6:5). The uncultivated branch has been cut off from the uncultivated tree, and this uncultivated branch is grafted into the cultivated tree, the good tree. The uncultivated branch is cut off from the original tree, and the cultivated tree is cut open. These two cuts are put together and grafting takes place. These two now become one, yet the branch is still the branch, and the tree is still the tree. They are two things, yet they live together. The branch and the tree live, but the two live together as one. The living of the branch and the tree is a mingled living. Their living is a mingling. To say that the grafted branch lives by the cultivated tree is not very accurate. The grafted branch lives in the cultivated tree and with the cultivated tree. Thus, the cultivated tree lives, and the grafted branch lives in the cultivated tree's living.

Some have mistakenly said that we Christians live an exchanged life. According to this concept, we exchange our poor life for a good life from Christ. This, however, is absolutely wrong. If our Christian life is an exchanged life, then our poor life is finished after being exchanged with the life of Christ. Although the Bible does say that we have been crucified, it also says that we still live (Gal. 2:20). When the Bible says that we have been crucified, this means that we have been cut off from Adam, the uncultivated tree. Through crucifixion we have been cut off from Adam, and in resurrection we have been grafted into Christ. We have been crucified, cut off, from Adam, and we have been put into the resurrected Christ. Therefore, we are not finished; we are still living. However, we are not living in ourselves, we are living in Christ, with Christ, and because of Christ, taking Christ as the factor for our living. When He lives, we live in Him. Our living is within His living; thus, our living and His living are mingled together as one living.

LIVING CHRIST
BY TAKING OUR SPIRIT AS OUR PERSON
WITH THE SOUL AS ITS ORGAN

The New Testament reveals that we have an old man (Rom. 6:6; Eph. 4:22) and that we are a new man (2 Cor. 5:17; Col. 3:10-11; Eph. 4:24; 2:15). Before we were saved, we were an old man without the new man. But after we were saved, we became a new man with an old man. Before we were saved, our soul was our person, and our spirit was merely an organ for us to contact and receive God. But when we were saved, receiving Christ as the life-giving Spirit into our spirit, our spirit became our new person, a new man. This new man is our regenerated spirit with Christ who is the life-giving Spirit, as its life. Our spirit has become our new person, and the soul has become an organ to serve our spirit.

Through regeneration our spirit received the divine life, making it a new man. Thus, our new man is the spirit, and our soul has become the organ of this new man. Our soul serves our spirit by its ability to think, understand, interpret, decide, love, or hate. All of these abilities are for the spirit's use, to serve the spirit's purpose. Our soul has been rejected as the person, but our soul is still useful as an organ for our new man, the regenerated spirit.

In order to live Christ, to live because of Christ, we must learn to deny our soul. The truth of denying the soul has been opposed by some. Some have said that if we deny our soul, we will be finished. To deny our soul, however, means to deny the soul as our person, but not as our organ. As an organ, our soul—our mind, emotion, and will—is very useful. In spiritual experience, the more spiritual we are, the more thoughtful we are. The more spiritual we are, the more emotional we are. Actually, if we do not know how to weep or shed tears, we are not very spiritual. However, we need to consider *how* we shed tears. If we shed tears from our soul as our person, this is not to live Christ.

For many years I never shed tears from my soul as my person. But when I began to live in the spirit, in my new man, taking the soul as my organ, I began to shed tears. At these times I shed tears by the soul as my organ, not as my person.

The person who shed tears was my spirit. It is the same principle today. When we love someone by our soul as a person, *then will*
that is wrong. It may be love, but it is of the old man and is *shed tears*
still related to the flesh. To love by our soul as our person *from our soul*
is wrong, but to love by our spirit as our person with our soul *as our person*
as our organ is right. It is impossible to love someone without
our soul. Our spirit, strictly speaking, does not have the
loving ability. In order to love, we must have a loving organ.
The loving organ is our emotion, a part of our soul.

Our spirit by itself cannot weep or shed tears. In the Gospels the Lord Jesus wept (John 11:35; Luke 19:41). He wept
from His spirit as His person with His soul as His organ. He
did not love by the soul as His person; rather, He loved by His
spirit as His person with His soul as His organ. Today, as
Christians, we are the same as the Lord Jesus. In our Christian life, our soul must be denied as our person, yet our soul
is still very useful as an organ. When our soul rises up to be
our person, we should tell our soul: "Dear soul, you were my
person in the past, but not today. Today, you are my organ in
resurrection, and my person is my regenerated spirit with the
Lord Jesus as its life. This spirit is the new man, and this new
man is my person. You, dear soul, are now only my organ.
Stay in your position, and do not propose anything to me.
When I love or think, you must be my loving and thinking
organ."

In my personal time with the Lord, my confession has
most often been about living from the soul as my person. Very
often I forgot that the soul was not my person, and I listened
to him. My soul told me to love, so I loved. I lived the old man,
not in doing bad things, but in doing good things. To merely
do good things is not to live Christ; it is not something of the
tree of life. Both good things and bad things are of the tree of
the knowledge of good and evil.

Only when we live Christ in our spirit are we living the
tree of life. We must ask ourselves each day whether we have
lived Christ or whether we have just behaved properly. Many
times I have confessed to the Lord, saying: "Lord, forgive me.
I still have not succeeded in living You. I lived You perhaps
only one fourth of the time. But the rest of the day, I lived the

old man by doing good. Paul could say, 'To me to live is Christ, and to die is gain,' but I cannot say this. Lord, forgive me."

QUESTIONS AND ANSWERS

Question: As unsaved people, we lived the old man. Now that we are saved, we live the new man. This seems to indicate that the old man is finished. How can we say that our old man, the soul, still remains as an organ? Romans 6 and 7 reveal that our old man was not only crucified with Christ, but also buried with Him. How can our soul, our old man, come back to be the organ of our new man?

Answer: We should not forget that Romans 6 does not stop at burial but goes on to resurrection (vv. 4-5). The crucified person was buried and resurrected. The natural faculties of our soul were crucified and buried, but they also were resurrected. We now have the faculties of our soul in resurrection. The soul as an organ of our new man, the spirit, is not in its natural condition. It is in a resurrected condition. Our natural man, our natural being, has been uplifted in Christ's resurrection. Our humanity has been crucified, buried, and uplifted by Christ's resurrection.

Question: As we have been crucified, buried, and resurrected, what was resurrected concerning us?

Answer: Before we were saved, our mind was very dull and foolish; our emotion was unrestricted and unbridled; and our will was either very stubborn or very weak. However, after we received Christ, He did not only regenerate our spirit, but He also uplifted our mind, emotion, and will through His resurrection. His resurrection immediately uplifted the natural faculties of our soul. Since we are saved persons, our mind, emotion, and will are surely different from the past.

Because we have been grafted into Christ, we are growing together with Christ, and the faculties of our soul are continuing to be uplifted and enriched. Romans 6:5 says, "For if we have grown together with Him in the likeness of His death, we shall be also in the likeness of His resurrection." To "have grown together with Him" is "to have an organic union in which the growth takes place that one partakes of the life and characteristics of the other. This is grafting (Rom. 11:24) that:

1) discharges all our negative elements; 2) resurrects our faculties created by God; 3) uplifts our faculties; 4) enriches our faculties; and 5) saturates our entire being to transform us" (Rom. 6:5, note 1—*Recovery Version*. See also Rom. 6:5, note 2).

Question: My concept has been that the life of the soul and the faculties of the soul are two different things. The life of the soul needs to be denied, but the faculties of the soul, including the mind, emotion, and will, need to be preserved. Is this an accurate understanding?

Answer: The life of the soul is the person, whereas the faculties of the soul are the soul as an organ. The soul is the organ, and the faculties of the soul are the abilities of this organ. It is better to say that we have the person of the soul and the organ of the soul.

Question: Our spirit contains the Spirit of Christ, who is a person with a mind, emotion, and will. How can we say that we do not have these faculties in our spirit?

Answer: Our spirit today is the new man, and in this new man, in this spirit, we have Christ as our life. Christ does have the faculties of loving, thinking, and deciding. However, the faculties of Christ are spiritual faculties, that is, they are the faculties of God. These divine faculties of Christ could only be manifested indirectly through our faculties. The faculty of Christ's thinking is never expressed directly by itself. It is always expressed through our mind (1 Cor. 2:16).

Adam was created according to God's image. Many Bible teachers define the image of God as the faculties of God to love, hate, and think. God loves, so we love; God hates, so we hate; God is very thoughtful, so we are thoughtful also. We have the image of God, yet this image remains empty without any content until we receive God. When we were without God, we exercised our minds in an empty way without God as the content in our mind. But when we receive God, God becomes our content. God's thinking becomes the content of our mind, and His love becomes the content of our emotion. A glove is a good illustration of this. The glove has five fingers, but these five fingers only have the image of the fingers, not the reality of the fingers. When the hand enters into the glove, then the fingers of the hand become the content of the fingers of the glove. Our mind, emotion, and will are just the fingers of the glove. When Christ comes into us with His mind, emotion, and will, His faculties become the very content of our human mind, emotion, and will.

Not many Christians understand these details of the spiritual life, but we need a vision of these details so that we can be those who live Christ.

THE EXPERIENCE AND GROWTH IN LIFE

MESSAGE FOUR

THE GROWTH IN LIFE

(2)

Scripture Reading: Gen. 1:26; Rom. 11:24; 6:5; Gal. 2:20

MAN AS A VESSEL AFTER GOD'S KIND

Life is the processed Triune God to be our destined portion. God created us as vessels that we might contain Him as our life. Without Him the created vessels are empty, having no portion, and their existence is a vanity. All thoughtful persons realize that their human life is vanity. Ecclesiastes was written by the experienced and wise King Solomon. In it he said, "Vanity of vanities; all is vanity" (Eccl. 1:2). Everything on earth is vanity of vanities because apart from God, man is empty. Man was made as an empty vessel in order to receive God as his portion, that is, as his life, life supply, and everything.

God created man in a marvelous way. Whether one has received God or is an atheist, not willing to receive Him, he must admit that man is the masterpiece of God's creation. The first items of God's creation were the things without life. Secondly, the things with the lowest life, the vegetable life, were created. They cannot speak or understand; they do not have a mind, emotion, and a will. Then a higher life, the animal life, was created. Among the animal lives, there are higher lives and lower lives. An insect's life is not as high as a dog's life, and a dog's life is not as strong as the lives of higher animals. However, the animal life is not the highest. The highest life in God's creation is the human life.

All living things are according to their own kind (Gen. 1:12, 24). The human life, however, is not according to the human kind but according to God's kind (Gen. 1:26). We are according to God's kind because we were made according to God, having God's image and God's likeness. Image refers to the divine attributes. God is loving; this is His image. Therefore, we also are loving. God is pure, and we were made pure, even though today we are fallen. God is in the light, and we desire to be in the light; we do not like to be in darkness. These are some of God's divine attributes. The attributes which we possess are the same as God's attributes, but the nature is different. God's attributes are divine; ours are not divine. What we possess is God's image. Therefore, man with his attributes is a vessel to contain God.

Likeness refers to the outward form. According to their appearance, man, the angels, and God are in one class. The angels look like human beings. After the Lord Jesus resurrected, His disciples came to His tomb, where they saw two men (Luke 24:4). Actually, those were not men but angels (John 20:12). On the one hand, the Bible tells us that God has no visible form. However, when He came to Abraham with two angels in Genesis 18, He appeared as a man (vv. 1-2). Abraham welcomed the three and prepared water for them to wash their feet. His wife prepared a meal, and they all ate, including Jehovah and the two angels. When Jehovah was leaving, Abraham accompanied Him, walking and talking with Him. In the form of a man, Jehovah talked to Abraham as an intimate friend (vv. 16-33; James 2:23).

THE GRAFTED LIFE

In order to grow in life, we need to see that the Christian life is a grafted life (Rom. 11:24; 6:5; Gal. 2:20). Two trees of diverse kinds cannot be grafted. They cannot grow together because they are not of one kind. Because man was created according to God's kind, man and God can be grafted together. If we are not clear about the principle of grafting, we will not be able to properly apprehend the matter of life. We will make mistakes related to life. Many Christians emphasize certain verses related to the Christian life, such as Romans 6:5 and Galatians 2:20. They feel that these verses refer to an exchanged life. However, the grafted life is not an exchanged life. The Christian life is a mingling of two lives, a life of two natures. Both lives still exist in the grafting.

Jesus was a fully grafted person, a person of two natures. On the one hand, when He lived on the earth He was the real God. On the other hand, He was a man expressing God. He was God expressed through man. We also are persons of two natures, the human and the divine. When we receive the divine life, our human life is not ended. Our human life still exists.

Even though the human and divine lives are of one kind, one is stronger than the other. We are now living by a weaker life with a stronger life. Whenever a weaker life is put with a stronger life, the stronger one subdues the weaker one. The sisters are the weaker vessels married to the brothers, who are the stronger vessels. For this reason, the wife takes the husband's surname as her own. In this sense, the wives are subdued. On their wedding day, the sisters realize this and put a covering over their head. During the wedding only the husband's head can be seen. This indicates that the two should live one life.

In the meeting we may joyfully proclaim, "I am a part of Christ, I am one with Christ, and I am mingled with Christ." However, after the meeting, we may desire to be the head and want Christ to be the covered one. We must always remember that we are the wife and He is the Husband. As such, we are two persons living one life together without separation. One lives in the other and through the other. This is the way the grafted life can come into being.

When we love, we do not love by ourselves. We love with Christ, through Christ, and in Christ, and Christ loves through us. This kind of love does not express our human virtue alone, but our human virtue with Christ's divine attributes. His divine love becomes the very essence of our human love. This is not two loves existing together, but one love living in the other. This can be compared to a hand in a glove. The hand and the glove are not two parties merely existing together. Rather, the hand is put into the glove, making the two objects one. When we are loving others, it is Christ who is loving, but not by Himself; Christ is loving through us. He is the "hand" and we are the "glove," not as a pair, but as one in the other. The human life has the divine life within it as its content, and the divine life has the human life as its expression. If this is not clear to us, we can never understand the Christian life.

Thank the Lord that there is such a thing as grafting. Hymn #482 in *Hymns* was written by A. B. Simpson, the founder of the Christian and Missionary Alliance. Verse three says:

> This the secret nature hideth,
> Harvest grows from buried grain;
> A poor tree with better grafted,
> Richer, sweeter life doth gain.

We must learn to see the grafted life and learn to exercise and practice it. We should not be joined with Christ as a pair. We must be joined to Him in the way of coinherence. He lives in us and we live in Him.

The Christian life is a grafted life, the mingling of two lives which are close in kind. To see this and practice it requires us to be in our spirit. We need to walk in life according to the spirit and do nothing without Christ. We should do everything with Christ and through Christ. If we do not have the assurance that we are doing something with Christ and through Christ, we should stop. This principle must be practiced throughout our entire Christian life.

THE EXPERIENCE AND GROWTH IN LIFE

MESSAGE FIVE

THE EXPERIENCE OF LIFE

(3)

Scripture Reading: Phil. 1:21; Rom. 8:6

In this message we want to continue our fellowship concerning living Christ.

THE MINGLING OF GOD AND MAN

The Bible, especially the Gospel of John, presents the divine and mysterious things in very simple words. John 14:19 says, "Yet a little while and the world beholds Me no longer, but you behold Me; because I live, you shall live also." The Lord Jesus spoke this word to let His disciples know that in resurrection He would be transfigured from His physical body of blood and flesh into the Spirit. In His resurrection He would live, and they would live also. This word itself is very clear, but the nature of our relationship with Christ is not so apparent from this word alone. This word spoken by the Lord implies the mingling of God and man.

The basic truth of the mingling of divinity with humanity is seen throughout the New Testament. Although some have condemned the use of the word *mingle,* the word *mingle* as defined by *Webster's Third International Dictionary* gives an accurate description of our relationship with the Lord. It states that to mingle is "to bring or combine together or with something else so that the components remain distinguishable in the combination."

LIVING CHRIST BEING A MINGLED LIVING

Philippians 1:21 says, "For to me to live is Christ, and to die is gain." To say that we must live Christ is easy, and to understand this simple phrase is also easy, but for us to actually live Christ involves a great deal. To live Christ means that when Christ lives, we who believe into Him and who are now in Him also live. Christ lives, and we live also (John 14:19). This means that we live in Christ's living and that He lives in our living. If we live in His living, His living will also be in our living. This is the mingled living of two lives. God and man live together. This mingled living is illustrated by the grafting of two trees. When a branch is grafted into another tree, the two live together as one. On the one hand, they are two, but on the other hand, they are one. They are one, yet their two natures remain distinct, and a third nature is not produced.

THE CHRISTIAN LIFE—LIVING CHRIST

In 1935 as a young co-worker, I stayed together with another co-worker who was a few years older than I was. During our stay together, I committed many small offenses toward him, so I apologized to him quite often each day. After a number of days, when I went to apologize to him again, he said, "To apologize is good, but not to offend is better." This disappointed me very much because I could not stop making offenses. One of my frequent offenses was to spill a few drops of water on his bed as I brought water from the rest room into our bedroom to wash myself. Actually, this was a very small thing, but according to my conscience, I had committed an offense, so I had to apologize. I practiced this according to the instruction I had received about keeping a conscience without offense toward God and man (Acts 24:16). I tried very much to practice this, but it was rather difficult. If I had been careless, I could have spilled a little water on the brother's bed without being bothered, but that kind of careless living or behavior kills our fellowship with the Lord. Although I exercised to keep my conscience void of offense, I had not been fully helped to live Christ.

Through many years of experience, I have learned that the Christian life is more positive than merely keeping our conscience void of offenses. We Christians should keep a clean conscience, but the main point of our Christian life is to live

Christ. To live Christ should be our goal. Whether our conscience is clean or not is secondary. Living Christ should be
primary. All the troubles in our Christian life come because of
our not living Christ.

To merely keep our conscience clean is to be in the realm
of morality and ethics. The practice of keeping my conscience
clean was a help, but it also became a snare. As I look back
on those early experiences, I now realize that morality and
ethics is not the Christian life. Today I would never stress
only the matter of keeping your conscience without offense;
rather, I would charge you to forget about all the other things
and live Christ. To me to live is Christ. To live is not ethics or
morality but Christ.

To a banker, to live is his money and the current interest rate. The interest rate is always on his mind, and he is
always looking at the newspaper to find out what the current
interest rate is. To a stockbroker, to live is the stock market.
To the young, ambitious college students, to live is to get the
highest degree in the best field. As a trainee in the training,
you may think that to live is the training. Actually, our living
should be Christ.

LIVING CHRIST BY LOVING HIM

As we are engaged in our daily activities, our living should
not be those activities, but Christ. Our mind should be concen-
trated on Christ, but this concentration of our mind depends
upon our love for Christ. This is why the New Testament
charges us to love Christ (Mark 12:30; Rev. 2:4-5; John 14:23;
21:15-17; 1 Pet. 1:8). If we do not love Christ, we cannot live
Him, and loving Him is the best way to concentrate our entire
being on Him. When a young mother delivers a child, her
whole living is that new baby. For her, to live is her new baby.
This is because of her love for her child. When we love Christ
to the uttermost, our entire being is occupied with Him, and
we live Him. This was Paul's experience; therefore, he said,
"To me to live is Christ, and to die is gain" (Phil. 1:21). To Paul,
to continue to live was Christ, and if he should die, it was gain.

Living Christ requires that we love Him to the uttermost.
Sometimes when we have been very captivated by something,

that night we would have a dream about that thing. Even in our dreams, for us to live was the thing that captivated us. Christ needs to captivate us to such an extent,

THE MIND SET ON THE SPIRIT BEING LIFE

Romans 8:6 says, "For the mind set on the flesh is death, but the mind set on the spirit is life and peace." In our practical Christian life, we must set our mind on the spirit. When we set our mind on the spirit, our mind is life. Life is God, Christ, and the Spirit. This life becomes real and practical to us when our mind is life. If our mind is not life, God and Christ as our life seem far away, and the Spirit is very objective to us. Christ is our life, but Christ as our life is practical to us when we set our mind on the spirit, and our mind is life. When our mind is set on the spirit, we have life.

THE MIND SET ON THE SPIRIT
BEING TO ABIDE IN CHRIST

To set the mind on the spirit is also to abide in Christ. When we abide in Christ, the issue, the result, is fruit-bearing. If we do not bear fruit, our abiding is false. If a married couple desires to have children and after a number of years does not have any, they may go to a medical doctor to find out what is wrong. We should not be deceived. Our abiding in Christ should produce fruit. Christ today is the Spirit (1 Cor. 15:45b; 2 Cor. 3:17), so we can now abide in Him. To abide in Christ, taking Christ as the Spirit, is to set our mind on the mingled spirit, our regenerated spirit. This proper abiding in Christ will surely result in fruit-bearing. Everyone who enjoys Christ will be charged by the Lord to go (John 15:16)! We are charged to "go forth" which implies that we should go some distance. We should not stay home, but we must go forth to bear remaining fruit. This is the result of abiding in Christ which is a matter of setting our mind on the spirit.

THE EXPERIENCE AND GROWTH IN LIFE

MESSAGE SIX

THE GROWTH IN LIFE

(3)

Scripture Reading: Rom. 8:1-6

FREED FROM THE LAW OF SIN AND OF DEATH

Being in Christ Jesus

Romans 7 speaks of our involvement with several persons. In this chapter there are a woman (vv. 2-3), two husbands (vv. 2-4), "I" (vv. 7-24), and sin (vv. 8-9, 11, 13-14, 17, 20). Chapter eight shows us another person. Verse 1 says, "There is now then no condemnation to those who are in Christ Jesus." We are now in Christ Jesus, not in the old husband, the "I," or sin. However, if in our experience we remain in the old husband or the "I," we are under sin. According to Romans 7, sin is a person (vv. 8, 9, 11, 17, 20). It is difficult to say whether this person is Satan or ourself, because these two are one. In Matthew 16 when Peter rebuked the Lord, saying, "God be merciful to You, Lord," Jesus turned and said to Peter, "Get behind Me, Satan!" (vv. 22-23). At that time, Peter and Satan were one. The "I" in Romans 7 is not merely identified with Satan; the "I" and Satan are one. Jesus Christ is the only person in the entire universe who is not one with Satan.

On the one hand, sin is Satan himself. On the other hand, because Satan injected himself into the human race, the entire human race also became sin, that is, the entire human race became one with Satan. In the eyes of God, Satan, sin, and the human race are one. If we live by the "I," we cannot avoid sin, because the "I" is sin. We can never get away from sin, and we can never overcome sin because we ourselves are sin. Regardless of how good one might seem to be in the eyes of others, in the eyes of God he is sin.

The experience of sin in Romans 7 leads us into condemnation (7:24; 8:1). The condemnation in Romans 8:1 is not the condemnation concerning the things we did in the past. It is the condemnation of our current situation. No one else condemns himself as much as a seeking Christian. Before we were seeking Christ, we did not condemn ourselves very much. After we had a clearance with God, we made up our mind to be perfect, pure, and right in everything. As a result, we may constantly condemn ourselves. Those who seek the Lord may not only be under this condemnation day after day, but even hour after hour. We condemn ourselves that we are wrong in our attitude and wrong in the way we speak, in the inaccurate words we use. If one means business to seek after Christ, he may become a person that constantly condemns himself. This is the condemned person unveiled in Romans 7 who eventually says: "Wretched man that I am! Who will deliver me from the body of this death?" (v. 24).

In Romans 7 Paul could not escape from sin. However, in chapter eight he declares, "There is now then no condemnation to those who are in Christ Jesus" (v. 1). Paul was no longer in himself. Therefore, he was not in sin, that is, he was not in Satan. He was in another person, Christ Jesus, who in our experience of life is the Spirit of life. Christ Jesus in verse 1 and the Spirit of life in verse 2 are one person. Without being the Spirit of life, Christ could not be real to us. In Christ we are freed from condemnation because Christ Jesus today is the Spirit of life.

The Law of the Spirit of Life

Romans 8:2 says, "For the law of the Spirit of life in Christ Jesus has freed me from the law of sin and of death." Strictly speaking, it is not the person of Christ in Romans 8:2 who frees us; it is the law of this person. With this person of life, there is a law, the law of the Spirit of life, that frees us from the law of sin and death.

Every life has a law and even is a law. Even the small insects know how to fly because of the law of their life. The

highest created life, the human life, is also a law. It is not correct to say that our sinful living comes from our habit. Our
living does not come from our habit; it comes from our life as
a law. If one scolds a table, it will not react, because inanimate things do not have a law. However, if we are scolded, we
will be angry due to the law of our natural life, which is ourselves.

(1) The law of the Spirit of life (Rom. 8:2), (2) the law of good in
the mind (7:23), and (3) the law of sin and death (7:23; 8:2) are
natural laws, not outward regulating laws. A natural law is
not a regulation; it is a natural power. Gravity is an example
of a natural law. When something is thrown into the air, it
comes down because of the law of gravity. Objects always fall
unless a stronger power is in effect. An airplane can fly
against the power of gravity only because the law of aerody-
namics overcomes the law of gravity. Without another power
to restrain us, we sin spontaneously, just as an object falls
downward when dropped. To tell a lie does not require exercise. When one lies, he does it spontaneously. Peter did not
need to exercise to lie when he denied the Lord, saying, "I do
not know the man!" (Matt. 26:72). He did it spontaneously.

Sin and death are companions. Where one is, the other is
surely there also. The law of sin is also the law of death. However, within us is a stronger person, Jesus Christ as the Spirit
of life. This stronger person is a stronger law, and this stronger law defeats us as the weaker law. In this way, the stronger
law frees us from the weaker law.

Setting Our Mind on the Spirit

We should no longer trust in ourselves and should not try
to overcome sin. We are not able to overcome it. Rather, we
should set our mind on the spirit. Romans 8:6 says, "For the
mind set on the flesh is death, but the mind set on the spirit
is life and peace." Today the Spirit, who is the Spirit of life,
Christ Jesus Himself, is one with us in our spirit. All day long
we need to set our mind on nothing but our spirit. Our mind
set on our spirit is life, and this life is the processed Triune
God—the Father, the Son, and the Spirit, the consummation
of the Triune God. Moreover, a person whose mind is set on

the spirit walks according to the spirit (Rom. 8:4). We must learn to see these truths and learn to practice setting our mind on our spirit all the time. This is the experience of life which produces the growth of life.

QUESTIONS AND ANSWERS

Question: Is the experience to which Paul refers in Romans 7 the experience of a believer or an unbeliever?

Answer: Romans 7 describes a fighting between two laws: the law of sin and the law of good. When we believed in the Lord Jesus, we were regenerated, and we became a new creation. However, after being saved every believer makes up his mind to do good. A new believer may say: "I was a sinful person in the past, but I have now repented and made confession to God, and I have believed in the Lord Jesus. Now since I am saved, I must try my best to do good." To make up one's mind in this way immediately brings one back to the experience of an unbeliever. When Paul wrote Romans 7, he was a saved person. After being saved, he may have gone back to his old standing as an unbeliever trying to keep the law. When a believer returns to the standing of an unbeliever under the law, trying to do good to please God, he experiences Romans 7.

Throughout the years Bible students have argued whether Romans 7 is the experience of an unbeliever or of a Christian. However, after being saved, every saved one experiences being brought back to the standing of an unbeliever. They make up their mind to please God, to do good, and to be perfect, but they are eventually defeated. In the morning they may have a morning revival, and after this revival they make up their mind to be perfect for the whole day. However, by noontime they have made several mistakes, and by the afternoon they may be fully defeated. That night they may try to make restitution, confessing their failures, and the next morning they will try again. This history repeats itself many times.

Question: Is trying to set our mind on our spirit an example of trying to do good?

Answer: In my youth I heard a saying, "To know sin is to sin." Before Adam and Eve took the fruit of the tree of the

knowledge of good and evil, they were innocent; there was no
sin. After they took the fruit, their eyes were opened, and
they began to know good and evil. To try to do good is sin.
Likewise, to try to set our mind on the spirit is also sin. Do
not try to do anything. Simply set your mind on the spirit.
Paul did not charge us to try to set our mind on the spirit. He
simply said, "The mind set on the spirit is life and peace"
(Rom. 8:6b). After hearing a message on setting the mind on
the spirit, some may resolve to do their best to do this. We
need to stop our doing. Whenever we try to overcome, we are
defeated. Faith is not doing or trying; faith is simply believing what God has said and saying "Amen." This faith keeps
us in rest.

Question: How do you apply the law of the Spirit of life?

Answer: To apply the law of life may also be our doing. Do
not consider how to apply the law of the Spirit of life or how to
stop the law of sin. If you have seen the law of the Spirit of
life, simply say, "Hallelujah, Amen!" The law of the Spirit
of life will work by itself; it does not need you to apply it.
Faith stops any kind of activity. It stops you from trying and
doing. We do not know how the Lord will do it, but we do
believe that He will do it.

Question: What is a practical example of setting our mind
on the spirit?

Answer: To define the way to set our mind on the spirit is
to yield to a temptation. Paul did not charge us by saying,
"Set your mind on the spirit." We do not need to make up our
mind to do this. Faith stops our activities. Faith always
praises God. The example of Joshua and Caleb in the Bible
shows us what it is to believe. Joshua and Caleb were not the
ones who overcame in Numbers 13 and 14; it was the One in
whom they trusted. God did everything. They simply enjoyed
what God did. In Joshua 3 they crossed the Jordan River, but
it was God who stopped the water. They simply walked over.

Do not try to overcome your sin. Simply believe. Hallelujah! We are in Christ. Christ is our great I Am, and He is
the Spirit of life. We have a Savior. If we do something for
ourselves, we are attempting to be our own savior. We are
declaring that we do not need Him. If we declare that we

are wretched and hopeless and cannot do anything to rescue ourselves, then we are declaring that we need a Savior.

Question: If in our fallen nature we are Satan, how can we live a grafted life with the Lord flowing through us to express Himself?

Answer: We are the branches grafted into the cultivated Christ. He is the stronger life, and we are the weaker life. Regardless of what Satan would do, Christ is stronger. As long as we abide in Him, we remain in the place where we are grafted. Christ will do everything. We do not need to analyze. An antibiotic is stronger than the germs. We know that it deals with the germs, but we do not know how, and we do not need to know.

Faith stops our activities. Faith even "blinds" us. If we have faith, we are like blind men. Abraham did not know where the Lord was leading him or what route he was taking. He only knew that the Lord was leading him. This is faith. To be too clear is to not believe.

Question: It seems that it is easy to have faith when I am in the meetings. However, as soon as I return home, there are "giants" waiting to devour what I have enjoyed. What can I do?

Answer: Faith is always real and true. The environment is a lie. Listen to faith, not to the lie. If our environment is good, we do not need to believe. We need to believe when we are in a difficult environment. Worry, anxiety, and even physical sickness, all are lies. Faith always tells the environment that it is a lie, not a giant. To deny the environment is faith. In Numbers 13 and 14, Joshua and Caleb took the word of God as their faith. The unbelieving Israelites all saw the giants in Canaan and gave an evil report. However, Joshua and Caleb said, "Only do not rebel against Jehovah; and do not fear the people of the land, for they will be our bread" (Num. 14:9). Do not recognize the environment. Do not say that the meeting hall is the mountain top and that your home is so poor. If you say this, you are standing with Satan. Your home is much better than the meeting hall. It is like the third heavens and the Holy of Holies, because wherever Christ is, there is the Holy of Holies.

Sometimes we help Satan to do many things. Our husband or wife may not be that bad, but because we say they are bad, they become bad. The more we talk in this way, the worse they will be. This kind of speaking opens the door to Satan. We need to shut the door by declaring something positive. We should say: "I am not defeated. My being defeated is a lie. Satan, this lie must return to you." To proclaim in this way is to exercise faith. Faith is against the environment.

Question: Some of the persons whom we are visiting are involved in improper matters. Should we tell them not to try to change themselves?

Answer: We should not tell them this. We should simply bring them into Christ. We need to help them to believe into Christ and to pray. The Lord Jesus did not tell Zaccheus to restore fourfold what he had taken from others. The Lord only ministered Himself into Zaccheus and did something within him. It was not Zaccheus himself who could give half of his possessions to the poor. It was the Lord within him. He experienced a dynamic salvation.

When we go to visit people, we must learn to speak Christ, to speak by the Spirit, that is, to minister Christ, the Spirit of life, into them. Then their salvation will be dynamic and organic, not something of teaching. Their salvation is not a receiving of a certain religion to change their way of living. Therefore, we have to pray much. While we are going out to speak to people we need to be praying: "Lord, regardless of how good my word is, it is vanity. You are the reality. While I am speaking, You must come out with my word."

Thank You Lord for speaking Yourself into me through the sister.
Lord, keep our sister walk by the Spirit still,
gain much more ones to be saved dynamically.

THE EXPERIENCE AND GROWTH IN LIFE

MESSAGE SEVEN

THE EXPERIENCE OF LIFE

(4)

Scripture Reading: Rom. 8:2, 6

Prayer: Lord, we need You. We need You Yourself every hour. Lord, anoint us with Your presence. Anoint the speaking and the listening with Your presence. Lord, apart from You we have nothing and we are nothing. Lord, we trust in You. Come in to meet our need. Amen.

In this message we want to continue our fellowship concerning Romans 8.

THE LAW OF THE SPIRIT OF LIFE

Romans 8:2, one of the most crucial verses in chapter eight, says, "For the law of the Spirit of life in Christ Jesus has freed me from the law of sin and of death." The main topic in this verse is not the Spirit of life but the law of the Spirit of life in Christ Jesus. Although a law is not a person, the law of the Spirit of life here is personified. The law of the Spirit of life frees us from the law of sin and death.

The phrase "the law of the Spirit of life" is composed of three things: the law, the Spirit, and life. "The law of the Spirit" means that the law is the Spirit. Other phrases with a similar grammatical construction are "the life of God" and "the light of God." The two nouns in such phrases are in apposition to one another. The life of God means the life is God, and the light of God means the light is God. When the Bible says "the Spirit of God" or "the Son of God," it does not mean that the Son and God are two separate persons or that the Spirit and God are two separate persons. The phrase "the Son of God" means the Son is God. In the same way, "the Spirit of God" means that the Spirit is God.

"The law of the Spirit" means the law is the Spirit. Likewise, "the Spirit of life" means the Spirit is life. The law is the Spirit, and the Spirit is life. All three nouns in this phrase are in apposition to one another. They do not refer to three separate things; rather, they are three aspects of one thing. Three things are compounded together as one.

The Spirit today is a compound Spirit typified by the compound ointment in Exodus 30, which was compounded with four spices and olive oil (Exo. 30:22-25). This ointment typifies the all-inclusive, compound, indwelling, life-giving Spirit. Without such types in the Old Testament it would be difficult to understand the different aspects of the one Spirit in the New Testament. The Spirit today is not only the compound Spirit but also the consummated Spirit. The consummated Spirit is the very consummation of the Triune God.

NEW TERMS TO MATCH NEW DISCOVERIES

In order to understand the Bible, we must learn many new biblical terms. According to biblical theology, many new terms such as *God's New Testament economy* have been introduced in the recent years. When I studied the Bible as a young man, I was warned by books I read not to invent any new terms in order to avoid heresy. However, I often received new light, which caused me to realize the need of new terms. Language develops according to the development of human culture. The words *vitamin* and *computer* are new terms which were invented to express some development in human culture. Theology today also needs some new terms because some new discoveries have been made. Therefore, I invented a number of new terms. There are many new terms in our theology. Brother Nee invented some, and over the past thirty years, I invented more.

THE TRIUNE GOD IN HIS DIVINE TRINITY
DISPENSED INTO THE TRIPARTITE MAN

The subject of Romans 8 is the Triune God in His divine Trinity dispensed into the tripartite man. In the entire Bible, only Romans 8 speaks about this very crucial subject. In verses 9 through 11, the terms "the Spirit of God," "the Spirit of Christ," and "Christ" are used interchangeably. This proves that the Spirit of God, the Spirit of Christ, and Christ are all one. Romans 8:9-11 reveals the Triune God.

Verse 10 says clearly that when Christ is in us, our spirit is life. In this verse there is also a comparison between our spirit and our body. Our body is dead, but our spirit is life. Concerning the body, the adjective "dead" is used, but concerning the spirit, the noun "life" is used. Our spirit is not just living or made alive, but our spirit is life itself. When the Triune God embodied in Christ came into us, our spirit became life. It not only was made alive but also became life itself.

Verse 6 shows that when the mind, the main part of our soul, is set on our spirit, it also becomes life. Then regarding our body, verse 11 says that if the Spirit of Him who raised Jesus from among the dead indwells us, He will also give life to our mortal body. Mortal means dying. The Spirit who indwells us will also give life to our dying body. Eventually, our dying body will also be life. These three verses show us that each of the three parts of our tripartite being become life. Our spirit has been made life, our mind, which is the main part of the soul, becomes life, and even our dying body will also be life.

In order to experience Christ as our spiritual life, we must know Romans 8 according to its subject: the Triune God in His divine Trinity dispensed into the tripartite man. Christ first came into us to make our spirit life. Hallelujah! This is regeneration, and it occurs in an instant. Some say that three minutes is too short a time for someone to be regenerated. Actually, three minutes could be too long. When electricity is installed in a building, the electricians prepare the wiring inside, and these wires are connected to a long wire that runs from the power plant to the building. Once the installation is complete, all that is needed is to turn on the switch. It is the same in preaching the gospel. The preparation of the wiring is our presentation of the gospel to our gospel friend. You may say, "Sir, you were created by God as a vessel to contain Him.

You are empty now without Him. God would like to come into you. Today He is Spirit. He is right here. If you open your mouth and say, 'O Lord Jesus,' believing in your heart that God raised Him from among the dead, He will get inside of you." Once he follows you to say "O Lord Jesus," he will be instantly regenerated. This is according to the truth of the gospel. In the denominations it may take three months or longer to regenerate one person. Then, to baptize him may take even a longer time.

Before going out to preach the gospel, we must be full of faith, believing in a thorough way. We must pray, exercising our faith with full assurance. Then when we go out, we have the divine electricity to impart Christ to people. This is not the mere preaching of the gospel but the impartation of Christ into people. Like the electrician who brings the electrical line into the building, we bring Christ into the lost ones.

The impartation of Christ into people for their regeneration was typified by the Lord imparting His resurrection life into the body of a widow's dead son (Luke 7:11-17). This was not the fact of regeneration, but it may be considered as a type of regeneration—the imparting of life into a dead person. The cases of Lazarus in John 11 and the dying child in John 4 indicate that fallen human beings are not only sinful but also dead. They need the impartation of life. When we go out to visit people with the gospel, our speaking of Christ is to impart life to them. We have to believe that we are not going merely to preach but to impart the living Christ who is life into people.

Immediately after we baptize someone, we need to give him a good message concerning the two spirits. We need to tell him that when we were regenerated in our spirit, our spirit was made life (Rom. 8:10). The regenerating Spirit who is life came into our spirit, becoming one with our regenerated spirit and making our spirit life. These two spirits have become one spirit (1 Cor. 6:17). This is not too deep for him. Such fellowship is the ABCs of the Christian life. Due to the shortage of today's Christianity, we may think that these things are too deep and mysterious. This is a mistaken concept. We simply need to learn how to speak these things. We must learn to appreciate the ability of the new ones. Their spirit was touched by us when we preached the gospel to them; otherwise, they would not have let us baptize them in their bathtub. It is not a small thing for a person to go to his or her bathtub to be baptized. We have to exercise our faith with full assurance.

When we preach the gospel in a proper way, our preaching is out of our experience of life. As we are preaching the gospel, we know with full assurance that Christ is in our spirit and that our spirit is life. Furthermore, when we are speaking Christ to sinners, our mind is definitely set on our spirit, and our mind is also life. We may be weak or sick in our mortal body, but when we speak Christ in the way of imparting Him into people, not only are our spirit and our mind life, but also our dying body is life.

Our experience of life is quite mysterious because our God is altogether a mystery. This mysterious One is now within us, making us a mystery. We are a mystery. Since we have this mysterious God within us, we should not think that we are so weak, unable to overcome sin such as our bad temper. The more that we say we cannot overcome, the more we cannot overcome. Regardless of our present situation, we always have to believe that we are able to overcome all kinds of situations. We must believe in all the positive things of Christ and not believe in defeat. The mysterious God operates by faith. Whenever we preach the gospel, we must exercise our spirit of faith (2 Cor. 4:13).

D. L. Moody said that the greatest miracle in the whole universe is regeneration. I agree with him. One moment someone may be a notorious sinner, and the next moment he may become a saint. The gospel we preach is powerful and dynamic. It is not mere doctrine in word. When we go to preach the gospel to others in a dynamic way, we are experiencing Christ, the Triune God, and life. To experience life is to experience the very Triune God dispensing Himself into our tripartite being. When we experience this dispensing, our spirit is life, our mind is life, and our body is also life.

THE EXPERIENCE AND GROWTH IN LIFE

MESSAGE EIGHT

THE GROWTH IN LIFE

(4)

Scripture Reading: Rom. 8:2, 10, 6, 11, 13, 4

PUTTING TO DEATH
THE PRACTICES OF THE BODY
BY THE SPIRIT

Romans 8 speaks about the processed Triune God as the Spirit of life (v. 2) dispensing Himself into the transformed tripartite man. When the Spirit of life, who is the consummation of the Triune God, enters into us, He enters into our spirit. By this He makes our spirit life (v. 10). Then when our mind, the main part of our soul, is set on the mingled spirit, our mind is also made life (v. 6). When this Spirit of life in our spirit reaches through our mind to our body, He gives life to our mortal body (v. 11). This is to make our body life.

Verse 13a says, "For if you live according to flesh, you are about to die." To live according to the flesh is to live according to what we are in our old man, whether it is good or bad. What we are in our old man may be very good. We may be someone who loves others. However, even if we love others, this love comes out from our old man. Paul did not say, "For if you live according to lust, you are about to die." Lust denotes the ugly and sinful things, the bad things of our old man. To drink wine excessively is according to lust. However, to drink a cup of pure water is not of lust, but it may still be out of our old man.

When the gospel was preached to us, we were dead persons (Eph. 2:1, 5; Col. 2:13) needing to be made alive. Because our self is death, if we live according to our self, regardless of what we do, we are about to die. To eat several meals a day is right, but most people eat according to their flesh, that is, according to themselves. The more they eat in this way, the more they die. According to their flesh, everyone is dying every day. The more they live, the closer they are to death.

Romans 8:13b says, "But if by the Spirit you put to death the practices of the body, you will live." We have to put to death the practices of our body. To put to death the practices of the body is to crucify them. We cannot do this by ourselves. We can only do it by the Spirit. One can kill himself in many ways, but one cannot crucify himself. Crucifixion must be carried out by another person. It is by the Spirit that we put to death the practices of the body. This means that we must hand ourselves over to the Spirit. We cannot crucify ourselves, but we can hand ourselves over to another One. This One is the one closest to us because He is within us. He is in our spirit, and to some degree He is also in our mind. He is within us, He is one with us, and we are one with Him. If we say, "I hand myself over to You, dear Lord," He will crucify us. This is not to be religious; it is not merely to pray and repent. By handing ourselves over to the crucifying Spirit, the killing Spirit, we are terminated. Then we will walk according to the spirit, and the Spirit who dwells in us will give life to our mortal body.

We must learn to experience Christ to such an extent that we would not even allow our body to do good things apart from the Spirit. When our body tries to do good things independently, we should say, "Lord, crucify the practices of the body." We should not go anywhere or do anything according to our flesh. Rather, we should have our being according to the spirit. We have to do everything, whether good or bad, according to the spirit. We should constantly hand ourselves over to the crucifying Spirit. Then we will be living, always enjoying Christ as life. Romans 8:4 says that we do not walk according to flesh but according to spirit. This is the issue of putting to death the practices of the body by the Spirit. Our walk includes all the items of our living, being, and thinking. We must do everything according to the spirit.

QUESTIONS AND ANSWERS

Question: Will saying, "Lord, I hand myself over to You" in whatever we are doing help us to learn the Lord in those things?

Answer: It is not necessary to speak so much. To hand ourselves over to the Lord is to abide, to remain, in the Lord (John 15:4). When we are abiding in the Lord, remaining in Him, we are handing ourselves over to Him. As long as we are remaining in the Lord, it is not necessary to say much. Just be simple, and remain in the Lord.

As fallen beings, we find it easy to be independent. This is our habit. When we are independent, we are not in the hand of the Lord. Still, because we are religious, we would not do wrong things. Rather, we may do many good things independently, even recklessly. There is nothing wrong with loving a brother, going to a meeting, or reading the Bible. However, we may do these things according to ourselves, independently of the Lord and not according to spirit. It is dangerous to be independent of the Lord. We should not care merely for where we are going or for what we are doing. We should care mainly that where we go or what we do is by and with the Spirit and not by ourselves.

Question: We have seen that we should follow the trained way in preaching the gospel, and we have also seen that we should be flexible. How do we reconcile these two ways?

Answer: They do not need to be reconciled. On our face, the eyes are the eyes and the nose is the nose. We also have a mouth with teeth and a tongue. We cannot "reconcile" them; they are what they are. When we hear a Christian teacher talking about the "tongue," we like to make every part of our face a "tongue." However, we still need the "eyes," the "nose," and the "ears." We have said that in visiting people, we have to form a team; we should not go by ourselves. We have to follow some regulations and not our opinion, and we are blessed if we go out in this way. However, it is very easy to do this in legality. Forming a team to go to people of the lower class is effective, but if we always go out in this way, we will gain only people of the lower class; we will miss the other classes of people. It may be that a middle or upper-class household will not open the door to a team. In this case we must change our way. We love all classes of people. We have to use different ways to gain different people. Our way to reach people must be flexible. The way we use in Taiwan is good for Taiwan, but it may not fit in America. All of us, especially the co-workers and the leading ones in all the churches, have to study the flexible way.

The Chinese have been very conservative for many centuries, but they have gradually changed their concept since coming to Taiwan. Today many Taiwanese merchants are very flexible. They can manufacture many things according to the patterns given to them. They do not produce things according to their own taste but according to the buyers' taste. They make clothing for South Americans according to the South American tastes, and they make clothing for northern Europeans according to the European tastes. We should not be so legal. If we are flexible, we will surely be able to touch any kind of person.

All human beings are reachable and touchable, but we must find a way to touch them. If we live in a neighborhood with a few men who are fond of fishing, it may even be necessary to go fishing with them. To go fishing without gaining fishermen as our goal is to fall into the world, but if we go to reach people, we will not be going fishing; we will be going preaching. After we go fishing with them three times, they will thoroughly open to us, and we will have an opening in their community. By this we can see that there are many ways to reach people. We should be flexible. There is a way to contact any kind of person.

Question: Is there literature available that categorizes people for gospel preaching and can help us to reach different kinds of people?

Answer: We have such material in Chinese that has not yet been translated into English. It is helpful in a general way, but if we rely on this too much, we may frustrate the Spirit. We must be desperate in gospel preaching because we will all stand before the judgment seat of Christ (2 Cor. 5:10). If we are not desperate, we will have a problem with the Lord both in this age and in the age to come. We must endeavor and be desperate to reach people to gain every kind of person. We have to pray that the Lord would burden the saints and make them desperate to gain people.

Question: After I preached the gospel to my employer, he was saved, but he has not gone on. Why is this?

Answer: We should not preach the gospel without coming to people. We must reach them and approach them. If we only preach the gospel to them, they may be saved, but if we do not come to them, they can never be fully brought to the Lord. We should first lay a good foundation by visiting them. It is inadequate only to invite them to come to the meeting hall. They can listen to a message, but even if they believe, they may still go away. The best way to approach someone is to go to their home. It makes a big difference if we go to their home to preach the gospel. Distributing tracts is not as effective as preaching the gospel by visiting people. To reach people by visiting them really works.

To reach people requires us to be absolute for gospel preaching. If we are teaching school, we are not merely teaching; we are living for Christ's preaching. This is what we are short of today. Thank the Lord that today there are many new ones among us because of the door-knocking, and some new churches have been raised up. In the past, when we insisted on bringing people to the meeting hall, we did not baptize many. However, in the new way, many people have been baptized. I hope that all of us would be stirred up to preach the gospel as priests of the gospel in the new way.

THE EXPERIENCE AND GROWTH IN LIFE

MESSAGE NINE

THE EXPERIENCE OF LIFE

(5)

Scripture Reading: Rom. 8:2, 10, 6, 11, 13

In this message, I will review the major points of the previous messages on the experience and growth in life.

LIFE BEING THE PROCESSED TRIUNE GOD

Life is God Himself, life is Christ, and life is the Spirit, but simply to say this is not adequate. Life is the processed Triune God. The God who is life to us is the processed Triune God. If God had never been processed in His Trinity, He would be life to Himself, but He could never be life to us. In order for God to be life to us, He had to be triune—the Father, the Son, and the Spirit.

As the Triune God, He was processed through several steps: incarnation, crucifixion, and resurrection. Without each of these steps, the Triune God could not be life to us. Incarnation is for the Father, with all His divine fullness, to be embodied in the Son (Col. 2:9) and through the Spirit (Luke 1:35) that He might have humanity added to His divinity. In incarnation the Son is the Father's embodiment, and the Spirit is the divine essence of the Son's incarnation. The Son is the embodiment of the Triune God with the Spirit as the essence.

The Son then went to the cross with the Father and through the Spirit. His going to die on the cross was not the Father's crucifixion nor the Spirit's crucifixion. It was the Son's crucifixion, yet the Son was not alone. He was crucified with the Father and through the Spirit. On the cross, Christ offered Himself to God through the eternal Spirit (Heb. 9:14).

The process of crucifixion is of the Son with the Father through the Spirit.

Resurrection is the Son's resurrection to become the life-giving Spirit (1 Cor. 15:45b). In resurrection, the Son became the Spirit (2 Cor. 3:17). The Son, the last Adam, became a life-giving Spirit in resurrection. The Son who died through the cross resurrected in the Spirit and as the Spirit.

These are the processes the Triune God passed through in order to be life to us. This life is the processed Triune God, the Son as the embodiment of the Father and the consummated Spirit as the consummation of the processed Triune God. Such a life is now embodied in the word. When the word reaches us, it is spirit and life (John 6:63). Now we have life. We have the Father, embodied in the Son, consummated as the Spirit, and embodied in the word, reaching us to be our life.

THE REVELATION OF LIFE IN ROMANS 8

The five crucial verses concerning life in Romans 8, verses 2, 10, 6, 11, and 13, unveil to us five crucial points, in the order of their significance, as follows:

The Law of the Spirit of Life

Romans 8:2 says, "For the law of the Spirit of life in Christ Jesus has freed me from the law of sin and of death." In this verse the phrase "the law of the Spirit of life" is composed of three elements. The order of these elements according to their significance is the Spirit, life, and the law. Without the Spirit, you cannot have life. Without life, the law is absent. The law comes out of life, and life is of the Spirit. In Romans 8 Paul did not say the Holy Spirit because "the Spirit" is understood to be the consummated Spirit. The Spirit in the New Testament denotes not only the Spirit of God and the Holy Spirit but also the consummated Spirit. The word *consummated* implies a process. Before something is consummated or processed, it may be raw. When food is uncooked, it remains raw, but once it is cooked, processed, or consummated, it is ready to be served at the dining table for people to eat. In the same way, the Triune God has been consummated. The

Spirit who is life to us is the consummated Spirit, the consummation of the processed Triune God.

The Spirit is the crucial element of the phrase "the law of the Spirit of life." "The Spirit of life" means that the Spirit is life and that life is the Spirit. The Spirit being the consummated God means that the Spirit is of God. God Himself is also Spirit (John 4:24). The Spirit is the essence of God, and He is also the consummation of God.

The law of the Spirit of life is not a law in letters, like the Ten Commandments, regulating us concerning good and evil. The law of the Spirit of life is like a natural law in physics. If you throw something into the air, it will drop to the ground. This is the law of gravity. The law of gravity is not a commandment in letters but a natural force, a natural law, which operates according to a principle. Romans 8:2-3 has two kinds of laws. The first law in verse 2 is the natural law. The second law in verse 3 is the written law, the law of Moses. Because of the weakness of our flesh, the written law had no possibility of doing anything for us, but the law of the Spirit of life as a natural law is just the divine life.

The vegetable life, the animal life, and the human life all have their own law. A life does not only have a law; a life is a law. When a tree is small, it may be hard to discern what kind of tree it is. As a tree grows, the kind of tree that it is becomes manifest. The almond tree will bring forth almonds, and the peach tree will bring forth peaches. The growth, shape, and fruit of each of these two trees is regulated by its own law. The almond life or peach life is the law.

The Spirit as the consummation of the processed Triune God is a law. He is life, so He also is a law. In verse 2 the Spirit is first in significance, life is second, and the law is last. However, in Romans 8 when life is applied, the law is first. In Romans 8:2 "the law" is the subject of the sentence and "has freed" is the predicate. The law of the Spirit of life has freed us from the law of sin and of death. This is not the law of Moses but the strongest natural law. It is the strongest law, because it is not merely God but the processed Triune God.

Before His process in eternity past (John 1:1), God was "raw," having only divinity. Through incarnation, the first step of His process, humanity was added to Him. After incarnation He is of two elements, divinity and humanity. Then He went to the cross and went through an all-inclusive death. The element of His death was then added to Him. Three days after His cruci-fixion, He entered into resurrection; thus, another element, resurrection, was also added to Him. Divinity, humanity, cruci-fixion, and resurrection all are the elements of the processed Triune God. As the "raw God," He was life only to Himself, but as the processed God, the "cooked God," He can be life to us. In resurrection He is the consummated Spirit, the consummation of the processed God to be life to us. This Spirit is called the Spirit of life. As the Spirit of life, He does not only have a law; He is a law. Today, it is this law that works in us.

Our Spirit Being Life

The next crucial verse in Romans 8 is verse 10, which says, "And if Christ is in you, though the body is dead because of sin, yet the spirit is life because of righteousness." In this verse, Christ is mentioned instead of the Spirit because the consum-mated Spirit is actually Christ Himself. When this Christ who is the life-giving Spirit is in us, our spirit becomes life.

Our Mind on the Spirit Being Life

In the initial stage of salvation, the inmost part of our being, our spirit, is made life. The other parts of our being are not yet life. Romans 8:6, another crucial verse, says, "The mind set on the flesh is death, but the mind set on the spirit is life and peace." From our spirit, the Spirit who is life spreads into our mind whenever our mind is set on the spirit. Our daily condition should be that our mind is on the spirit. We must be such a people who always have our mind on nothing but the spirit. In order to live, we must have our mind on something. Our mind on the spirit is life. This is transforma-tion.

Life to Our Mortal Bodies

The fourth crucial verse is Romans 8:11, which says, "But if the Spirit of Him who raised Jesus from among the dead dwells in you, He who raised Christ Jesus from among the dead will also give life to your mortal bodies through His Spirit who indwells you." In this long verse, all Three of the divine Trinity—the Father embodied in the Son in incarnation, the crucified Son, and the Spirit in resurrection—are applied. When the divine Trinity is indwelling us, this One gives life to our mortal bodies. Eventually, this will consummate in the transfiguration, redemption, and glorification of our bodies (Rom. 8:23, 30; Phil. 3:21).

Romans 8 unveils God's salvation in three steps. The first step enlivens our spirit (v. 10). The second step enlivens our mind (v. 6), the main part of our soul. The last step enlivens our dying body (v. 11). This makes our entire being—spirit, soul, and body—life.

The Application of God's Salvation

The last crucial verse shows the application of this salvation. Romans 8:13 says, "For if you live according to flesh, you are about to die; but if by the Spirit you put to death the practices of the body, you will live." This is the conclusion. The processed Triune God is now ready. All that is needed for us to do is to "come and dine." To come and dine is to apply this salvation. The way to apply this salvation is not to have our being according to the flesh but to live according to the spirit. The spirit mentioned in verse 13 refers to the mingled spirit; therefore, it should not be capitalized. This spirit is the human spirit mingled and saturated with the consummated divine Spirit. We should live according to such a spirit.

In verses 5 and 6 there are two important things, the flesh and the spirit. The crucial point in our application of God's provision is to live according to the spirit. If we live according to the flesh, we are about to die; but if we live according to the mingled spirit, we shall live. The unbelievers have only the negative provision of the flesh. We Christians, however, have both the negative provision of our flesh and the positive provision of the mingled spirit. The negative provision came from our fall, and the positive provision came from God's salvation. We are now in the middle, and the outcome of our life depends upon our choice. If we live according to the flesh, we die. If we live according to the spirit, we live. This means that our entire being—our spirit, soul, and body—lives.

QUESTIONS AND ANSWERS

Question: Since the Lord Jesus said in John 11:25 that He is the resurrection, what does it mean that the element of resurrection was added to the Triune God? What is the difference between His being resurrection and the element of resurrection being added into the Triune God in resurrection?

Answer: In the human mind, there is the element of time. We always ask what is first, second, or last, but in the divine realm, there is no element of time. A circle is often used to illustrate eternity or eternal things because it has no beginning point or ending point. If we were to mark two points on the circumference of the circle indicating Christ's crucifixion and resurrection, it would be difficult to say which occurred before the other. According to Revelation 13:8, Christ was crucified from the foundation of the world. This means that at the time the world was founded, Christ was crucified; but according to our mind, the crucifixion of Christ occurred a long time after the foundation of the world. This is the way our mind considers because of the element of time.

According to the divine concept, there is no element of time; there are only facts. When the incarnation, crucifixion, and resurrection occurred in time makes no difference in the divine realm, which is outside of time.

Question: What is it to set our mind on the spirit?

Answer: First, it should not be a matter of setting our mind on the spirit; it should be a matter of our mind being on the spirit. Second, we must have a clear view that we are fallen people who have been saved; therefore, we have two kinds of provisions. The first is the negative provision of the old man, and the other is the positive provision of the new man, the mingled spirit. The old man is signified and represented by the flesh. The new man is signified and represented by the spirit. If we live and have our being according to the flesh, the mind is on the flesh. If we live according to the spirit, our mind is on the spirit. If we try to set our mind on the spirit, this indicates we are not living according to the spirit. If you are living according to the spirit, your mind is spontaneously on the spirit. In this kind of condition, you are living. If you are not in this condition, you are about to die.

Question: What does it mean to be according to the flesh or according to the spirit?

Answer: To analyze or to explain what it means to live according to the spirit is hard. We may not be so clear that we are living according to the spirit, but we know for certain when we are living according to the flesh. As long as we know that we are living according to the flesh, we know that we are not living according to the spirit.

OUR NEED OF A CLEAR VISION OF LIFE IN ROMANS 8

If you receive a clear vision of life from Romans 8, you are in the experience and growth in life. When I was a young Christian, I read the Bible many times, and I tried to discover how to grow in life. Eventually, I realized that the answer is implied in all the different items of the divine theology in the New Testament. This is the reason I have presented the experience of life and the growth in life as I have done in these messages. Our need is to see a vision of the experience of Christ. As you read these items of the divine theology again and again, one day you will be enlightened to see clearly how to experience Christ. We may have learned the theology of the recovery, but our need is for this theology to become our vision. When you have a vision, there is no need to merely recite these things; rather, you can just point out to people what you see of the divine scenery according to the divine view.

To give a message on the matter of life is very, very hard because life is a spontaneous thing. Suppose there is a little tree growing in front of me. If I do not touch it, it really grows, but when I touch it, the growth is bothered. It may be better not to touch it. It is the same when I fellowship with you concerning the experience of life. When I encourage you to experience life, you may not experience life. To experience life is like switching on electricity which has been installed in a building. When you need electricity to go to a lamp, you simply go to the switch, turn it on, and the light comes on. When you turn the switch off, the electricity stops, and the lamp no longer has any light. Your experience of life is the same. When you sense that the light has been turned off, you need to pray, but your prayer may also be a problem. If you pray, "Lord, set my mind on the spirit," this prayer may not work. You should pray by allowing the interceding Spirit within you to pray by groaning (Rom. 8:26). By this kind of prayer, the switch is turned on again.

Before we came into the Lord's recovery, we might not have had any knowledge concerning the switch of the mingled spirit. Sometimes we accidently turned the switch on and just as quickly turned it off again. Today, however, in the Lord's recovery, we are not in that much darkness. We have realized that Christ is the Spirit in our spirit and that this Christ is the consummated Spirit. When He is here, life is here. Now, we have to live according to this life. Just to know this much will turn the switch on. Our problem is that we do not remain here. We need to come back and pray. In our prayer, it is better not to say too much. We should simply groan. Soon the switch is turned on again, and we are also happy again.

Romans 8 shows us a heavenly vision with view after view. Nearly every verse is a view. Verse 2 is a view to show you how the consummated Triune God today is life to you, and this life is a law. Verse 10 shows you another view of the consummated Triune God as Christ in your spirit. Now, your spirit is life. Verse 6 presents another view concerning the mind on the spirit. Then verse 11 presents the view that the Spirit of life as the processed Triune God indwells you to give life to your body. You then become a person of life. You are life in your spirit, you are life in your mind, your soul, and you are life in your body. Once you see all these views, you then need to apply them. Whether you are about to die or live depends upon whether you live according to the flesh or according to the spirit. We must learn not to live according to the old man, the flesh, but to live according to the spirit, the new man.

THE EXPERIENCE AND GROWTH IN LIFE

MESSAGE TEN

THE GROWTH IN LIFE

(5)

Scripture Reading: Heb. 4:12-16

Romans 8 reveals the processed Triune God dispensing Himself in His divine Trinity into the tripartite man. First, Christ comes into our spirit to make our spirit life (v. 10). Then from our spirit, He spreads to our mind to make our mind life (v. 6). Third, the processed Triune God consummated as the Spirit indwells us, making our mortal body life (v. 11). The goal of the processed Triune God is to dispense Himself into the three parts of our being. The very center of our being is our spirit. Our spirit, which was deadened (Eph. 2:5; Col. 2:13), was regenerated and made alive, even becoming life. The indwelling One, Christ as the embodiment of the processed Triune God, spreads from our spirit to our mind, and through our mind reaches our dying body.

Hebrews 4 contains the application of the revelation in Romans 8. According to our life experience, Romans 8 and Hebrews 4 speak concerning the same thing. Romans 8 is from the viewpoint of our spirit, while Hebrews 4 is written from the viewpoint of the heavens. By putting these two ends together, we can have a clear view of the divine revelation. The link between our spirit at one end and the heavens at the other end can be compared to Jacob's dream at Bethel (Gen. 28:10-19). "Bethel" means the house of God. Genesis 28:12 says, "And he dreamed, and behold a ladder set up on the earth, and the top of it reached to heaven: and behold the angels of God ascending and descending on it." We can see the ladder between earth and heaven again in John 1:51. The Lord Jesus said to Nathanael, "Truly, truly, I say to you, you shall see heaven opened and the angels of God ascending and descending on the Son of Man."

THE DIVIDING OF SOUL AND SPIRIT

Hebrews 4:12 says, "For the word of God is living and operative and sharper than any two-edged sword, and piercing even to the dividing of soul and spirit, both of joints and marrow, and able to discern the thoughts and intents of the heart." In order to apply the revelation in Romans 8, our soul must be divided from our spirit. We must discern the distinction between our soul and our spirit. The way to have this discernment is through the word. After reading a portion of the Bible in the morning, the division of our soul and our spirit will be taking place within us, even without our knowledge. Even if what we read does not mention the soul and the spirit, we will begin to sense that certain things within us are soulish, of our self and not of Christ. Some who love the Lord and love the Word may not know the proper teaching concerning the dividing of soul and spirit. But simply by reading the Word, their soul is divided from their spirit.

When Paul wrote the book of Hebrews, many Hebrew believers were lingering on the border between Judaism and God's New Testament economy. They were hesitating and wondering in their mind. In Hebrews 4 Paul showed the believers how to have their soul divided from their spirit through the reading and understanding of the Word. By taking the word, they were able to see that they should come out of Judaism and follow their spirit and not their soul.

Verse 13 says, "And there is no creature that is not manifest before Him, but all things are naked and laid bare to the eyes of Him to whom we are accountable." In human society today, many things are confused, but before God nothing is confused; everything is clear and divided. When we come into the church, we begin to be divided. We learn to discern the difference between our soul and spirit, and we learn to discern our intents and thoughts. If we learn to discern, nothing about us will be confused; everything will be clear. When we speak a wrong word with our wife, we will immediately know that our word came from the soul. Sometimes after reading the Word, a husband may come to his wife and say: "I am sorry. I was too much in myself in the way I dealt with you." On the other hand, if we do not love the Lord and are far away from Him, we will not be able to discern the source of our words.

The word of God is living and operative. As the word operates in us, it even has a way to heal our body. Proverbs 4:20-22 says: "My son, attend to my words; incline thine ear unto my sayings. Let them not depart from thine eyes; keep them in the midst of thine heart. For they are life unto those that find them, and medicine to all their flesh" (Heb.). The word is medicine even for our physical body. Many lovers of God can testify that the more they read the Word, the healthier they become. If we are able, it is a healthy practice for us to fast for one meal a week. Instead of eating physical food at that time, we can eat the word of God (Jer. 15:16). When we fast, we should attach ourselves to the word of God. The word of God will make us healthy because it is living and operative.

THE GREAT HIGH PRIEST

Verse 14 says, "Having therefore a great High Priest who has passed through the heavens, Jesus, the Son of God, let us hold fast the confession." In Romans 8 the One who indwells us is Christ. In Hebrews 4 the One who approaches God is the High Priest. At our end, He is Christ coming to us from God; at God's end, He is the High Priest going to God for us. Ascending, He is the High Priest, and descending, He is Christ. After His resurrection, He ascended from the earth. To the disciples it seemed that He was leaving them. However, His going from the disciples was for His coming back to them (John 16:5-7). His ascending was for His descending.

The angels in Jacob's dream were not first descending and then ascending. They first ascended (Gen. 28:12), rising from the earth to reach God. After His resurrection, Christ did not come directly to dwell in His disciples. On the morning of the resurrection, Jesus told Mary, "Go to My brothers and say to them, I ascend to My Father" (John 20:17). Then in the evening, Jesus came to His disciples and breathed the Spirit into them (v. 22). This was His descending to enter into them. The ascending was in the morning, and the descending was in the evening. First, He ascended to the heavens to present Himself to God in the freshness of His resurrection to satisfy the Father. Then He descended to the disciples in order to enter into them to be their life and their everything for their satisfaction.

COMING FORWARD TO THE THRONE OF GRACE

According to the Old Testament type, the high priest ministered in the Holy of Holies. Within the Holy of Holies there was the ark, and upon the ark there was the propitiation cover, or mercy seat (Exo. 25:17, 21), upon which the propitiating blood was sprinkled. This seat signifies the throne of God, which is the throne of authority to all the universe (Dan. 7:9; Rev. 5:1) but the throne of grace to us, the believers (Heb. 4:16). Moreover, it is the throne of God and of the Lamb, Christ (Rev. 22:1). God and the Lamb sit on the one throne in the way of coinherence, in the way of being two yet one.

Today the throne of God is both in our spirit and in the heavens. This may be illustrated by electricity. Electricity is both in the power plant and in our homes at the same time. Christ is both in the heavens and in our spirit, and where Christ is, there is the throne of God. Just as the one electricity joins the power plant to our home, the Christ who is in the heavens is also within us, joining us with the heavens and bringing the heavens down to us, making us one with the heavens. Today we are in the heavens, and the heavens are in our spirit.

Hebrews 4:16 says, "Let us therefore come forward with boldness to the throne of grace, that we may receive mercy and may find grace for timely help." The way to come forward to the throne of grace is to turn to our spirit. To turn to our spirit, we do not need to pray much. When we simply say, "O Lord," we have the sensation that the throne of grace is within us. Today in our spirit there is heaven, the throne of authority, and the throne of grace with God and the Lamb. When we call on the Lord, we are in our spirit, and our spirit is in the heavens with the throne of authority, the throne of grace, and the coinhering God sitting on the throne. This is the way to apply Romans 8.

Every day we should continually come forward to the throne of grace. This is the real experience of life. Whenever I am going to speak in a meeting, regardless of how busy I am, I spend at least five minutes with the Lord. When I call on the Lord, I am in my spirit, and I meet Christ on the throne of grace. In this way, I receive mercy and find grace for timely help. Then I can speak with the heavens and with the throne of grace and the coinhering God on the throne. To speak in this way is to speak in the enjoyment. The more we speak in this way, the more we enjoy the heavens, the throne of grace, and the very coinhering God.

After seeing the revelation in Romans 8, we need to come to Hebrews 4. First, we must discern our soul from our spirit. Then we need to experience the indwelling Christ and the High Priest going to God for us. Then we will receive mercy and find grace.

THE EXPERIENCE AND GROWTH IN LIFE

MESSAGE ELEVEN

THE EXPERIENCE OF LIFE

(6)

Scripture Reading: Phil. 1:20-21; 2:5-16; 3:12, 14; 4:10, 12-13

THE EXPERIENCE OF CHRIST

The New Testament unveils Christ, and every book in the New Testament is for the experience of Christ. The experience of Christ is the key which opens up each book of the New Testament. In this message we shall consider the experience of Christ in the book of Philippians.

THE FURTHERANCE OF THE GOSPEL BEING THE FACTOR FOR LIVING CHRIST

The experience of Christ unveiled in the book of Philippians includes several items. In chapter one Christ is our life and living. To take Christ as our life within and our living without is to live Christ (v. 21a). This chapter also reveals that the reason we live Christ, taking Christ as our life and our living, is for the furtherance of the gospel (vv. 5, 12). The experience of Christ as our life and living comes out of the furtherance of the gospel. The more we have fellowship in the gospel, in coordination with the apostle, the more we live Christ. The factor for living Christ is the furtherance of the gospel which is carried out in a corporate way.

Some have separated the preaching of the gospel from the experience of Christ. This is a mistaken concept. Our experience of Christ, our living of Christ, must have the factor of the furtherance of the gospel. Without such a factor, our words about living Christ are vain. Paul and the Philippians lived Christ, taking Christ as their life within and their living without, because they all were in the corporate fellowship of the gospel. The apostle was burdened for the furtherance of the gospel, and the Philippians were in coordination with him. Paul and the Philippians were happy in the furtherance of the gospel, and they all enjoyed Christ as their life within and their living without. Philippians 1 reveals not only the factor but also the result. The factor is the furtherance of the gospel with the apostle, and the result is the enjoyment of Christ, the experience of Christ, as both our life within and our living without. When you go out in the gospel, you enjoy Christ not in a doctrinal way but in a very experiential way.

Some have said that we should not have too much activity but that we should learn to enjoy Christ by attending the meetings, doing our best to uplift the meetings so that others may enjoy Christ. But without the factor of the furtherance of the gospel, we cannot enjoy Christ that much. Some have also said that we should come back to the enjoyment of Christ, implying that the preaching of the gospel is not the enjoyment of Christ. Our enjoyment of Christ must have a factor, and it must also have an issue. The furtherance of the gospel is the factor of our enjoyment of Christ. Furthermore, the more we enjoy Christ, the more we participate in the furtherance of the gospel. Thus, the furtherance of the gospel is also the issue of our enjoyment of Christ.

The enjoyment of Christ will cause you to visit people in their homes with the gospel. The enjoyment of Christ will never make you sleepy; rather, it will stir you up. When we enjoy Christ to the uttermost, we are beside ourselves. The more we enjoy Christ, the more active we will be. When we enjoy Christ, we can never be silent or quiet.

Paul enjoyed Christ to such an extent that he could say, "For to me to live is Christ, and to die is gain" (Phil. 1:21). The "gain" here is the presence of Christ. To live is Christ, and to die is to enjoy the presence of Christ. Paul might have said: "According to my feeling, I would rather die, because to die is to be present with the Lord. Nothing on the earth can satisfy me any longer, but if I die, I will be with Christ. This is much better for me; but for your sake, Philippians, I choose to remain here in order to live Christ, to impart Christ, and to share Christ with you."

I dare not compare myself with the Apostle Paul, but in my experience I have had the same kind of feeling that he expressed in Philippians 1:21-24. As an elderly person, I have had a lot of experiences on this earth. I have lost my taste for anything on this earth except Christ. As a young person it is easy to be attracted to other things. But, as an elderly man, without the Lord Jesus, I would lose interest in living. This is because there is nothing good on this earth. The only interest, taste, and enjoyment I have as I remain on this earth is to help sinners receive Christ, to help all of you enjoy Christ more, and to help the church be built up organically as the living Body of Christ. This is what I really enjoy.

During these last five weeks of the training, I have been quite busy laboring even until late at night. Yet, I have had a good and sound sleep every night. Occasionally, the enemy Satan raises up attacks from different directions, but the Lord has taught me the lesson of not being touched or stirred up regardless of what happens. I can testify that nothing on this earth can frustrate someone who enjoys Christ. Paul's experience was like this. Paul wrote his Epistle to the Philippians from a prison in Rome while he was under the threat of martyrdom. He knew that he might be killed, but he was not bothered or upset; rather, he expected to magnify Christ in his body through life or through death. He said this while his body was in bonds. His concern was not for his bonds but for how the enjoyment of Christ among the Philippians could be increased. When the material gift came to him from the Philippians (4:10-17), he was happy because this indicated that their concern for the furtherance of the gospel, which had become dormant, was blossoming again. Their experience of Christ made him very happy.

CHRIST AS OUR PATTERN AND EXPRESSION

The subject of chapter two is taking Christ as our pattern (Phil. 2:5-11) and experiencing Christ as our expression (Phil. 2:12-16). When we take Him as our pattern, spontaneously we express that pattern.

CHRIST AS OUR GOAL AND SEEKING

In chapter one Christ is our life and our living, in chapter two Christ is our pattern and our expression, and in chapter three Christ is our goal and our seeking, our pursuit (vv. 12, 14). We all must have a goal, and our goal must be Christ. He is our seeking, our pursuit. Day after day we seek Christ. He is not only our destination but also our goal. Sometimes we may reach a certain destination but miss our goal. In shooting a gun, the bullet may reach the target, but it may not touch the center of the target. We have to run not only to reach the destination but to obtain the goal.

CHRIST AS OUR STRENGTH AND SECRET

In chapter four Christ is our strength (v. 13) and our secret (v. 12). Paul said, "I can do all things in Him who empowers me" (v. 13). In order to do anything, we need strength, and we also need to know the secret, the way, to accomplish a task. You may have a lot of strength, but if you do not have the secret, you may waste your strength. Even in tasks such as arranging plants in a house or hanging pictures on the wall, there is a certain way, a secret, to doing them. Christ is not only our strength so that we are able to do things; He is also our secret. A secret is not rigid or legal but very flexible. It is always flexible and readily available to be applied at any time and at any place.

EXPERIENCING CHRIST
THROUGH THE BOUNTIFUL SUPPLY
OF THE SPIRIT OF JESUS CHRIST

As Christians, we should enjoy Christ as our life, our living, our pattern, our expression, our goal, our seeking, our strength, and our secret. The way for us to enjoy and experience Christ as all of these items is through the bountiful supply of the Spirit of Jesus Christ (Phil. 1:19). The Spirit in this verse is called the Spirit of Jesus Christ. This Spirit is the consummated Spirit. In eternity past the Triune God had not passed through any processes. But in time, the Triune God passed through incarnation, human living, crucifixion, and resurrection. After all these processes, He became a life-giving Spirit (1 Cor. 15:45b), the consummated Spirit. This consummated Spirit is the consummation of the Triune God. Now, after all the processes, God is no longer "raw." He has been processed, "cooked." This "cooked" Triune God as the Spirit is the consummation of the Triune God.

After His resurrection and before His ascension, the Lord Jesus came back to the disciples and said, "Go...disciple all the nations, baptizing them into the name of the Father and of the Son and of the Holy Spirit" (Matt. 28:19). In the entire Bible, this is the first time the Triune God is mentioned in such a perfect and complete way. At this time, after resurrection, the Triune God had been consummated. In eternity past He was the Triune God, eternally perfect but not complete. He did not have the human nature and the experiences of human living, death, and resurrection. Through incarnation He put on human nature; thus, humanity was added to His divinity. He then passed through human living. That was wonderful, but He still had not experienced death. He entered into death and died an all-inclusive death, solving all the negative problems in this universe. From that time onward, the element of death has been with Him. Death in Adam is ugly, but the death accomplished by Christ is so dear, precious, sweet, and lovable. Now such a sweet death is with the Triune God.

After His resurrection, He came back to His disciples and breathed into them the consummated Spirit (John 20:22). This Spirit is not only the Spirit of God, but also the Spirit of Jesus (Acts 16:7), and the Spirit of Christ (Rom. 8:9). This Spirit as the consummated Spirit, the all-inclusive Spirit, is the consummation of the processed Triune God. Such a Spirit is now within us. The Triune God—the Father, the Son, and the Spirit—is now in us (Eph. 4:6; 2 Cor. 13:5; Rom. 8:11). If we want to enjoy Christ and experience Christ, there is no other way except by the all-inclusive Spirit as our bountiful supply.

Paul said the Spirit of Jesus Christ had become his salvation (Phil. 1:19). From what did this Spirit save him? This Spirit did not save him from his bonds or chains; rather, this Spirit saved him from being weak, so that he could magnify

Christ. By this Spirit, Paul in his imprisonment was able to magnify Christ without being defeated. This is salvation on the highest level. If we were taken by persecutors and threatened with death, we might pray, "Lord, save me from being martyred." This kind of prayer indicates that we are already defeated. Instead, we should pray, "Lord, supply me with the bountiful supply of the Spirit of Jesus Christ that I may overcome such martyrdom." This would be salvation on the highest level.

When I was a young Christian, my friends and relatives who did not love Christ would sometimes argue with me, saying: "Look at how much the Apostle Paul loved Christ. Did Christ save him from Roman imprisonment? Did Christ save him from being martyred? You should not believe in Him or love Him because He cannot be seen, and He can do nothing for you. Jesus Christ did nothing for the Apostle Paul, and he was martyred. Where is your salvation?" This salvation may not deliver us from martyrdom; rather, it gives us the victory in martyrdom.

In the 1930s as the Communists were spreading in China, they captured and martyred two missionaries. One of them said that the face of a martyr is an angel's face, and his heart is a lion's heart. This missionary experienced salvation to the uttermost. The Apostle Paul also enjoyed Christ even in the face of martyrdom through the bountiful supply of the Spirit of Jesus Christ. Paul might have prayed: "Lord, thank You that You have chosen me, commissioned me, and sent me. Caesar did not bring me here, but You have brought me here. Lord, I am willing and ready to be martyred. What a glory that I can die for You." The Spirit of Jesus Christ became Paul's top salvation.

We may have all kinds of situations in our married life, work life, and in our relationships with other brothers and sisters. These situations may cause us to be defeated. The only way not to be defeated is by the bountiful supply of the Spirit of Jesus Christ.

You may be without a job. If you pray for a job and the Lord gives you a job, you may be happy and say that your getting a job is your salvation. Actually, this is not salvation. On the other hand, suppose you lose your job and, being unable to find a job, have to look for two or three months. If you have the strength to overcome the suffering of losing a job in order to live and magnify Christ by the bountiful supply of the Spirit of Jesus Christ, this is the top salvation.

Although the term *the Spirit* is short and simple, it denotes something which is all-inclusive. The Spirit is the secret of our victory. In human life, one of the most difficult things is to forgive people. To remember someone's mistake is easy, but to forgive someone's mistake is hard. To forgive means to forget. To forgive anyone's offense to the extent that you forget requires the bountiful supply of the Spirit of Jesus Christ.

By this Spirit you take Christ as your life for your living. By this Spirit you take Christ as your pattern for your expression. By this Spirit you take Christ as your goal and your pursuit in seeking. By this Spirit you are really able to do all things in the One who strengthens you, and this is your secret.

THE EXPERIENCE AND GROWTH IN LIFE

MESSAGE TWELVE

THE GROWTH IN LIFE

(6)

Scripture Reading: Phil. 3:7-10

Philippians 3:7-9 says: "But what things were gains to me, these I have counted loss on account of Christ. But surely I count also all things to be loss on account of the excellency of the knowledge of Christ Jesus my Lord, on account of whom I have suffered the loss of all things and count them refuse that I may gain Christ, and be found in Him, not having my own righteousness which is of the law, but that which is through the faith of Christ, the righteousness which is of God based on faith." To be found in Christ is a great matter. We are in Christ, but it is possible that people do not find us in Him. There are many millions of Christians in America, but we may not often be able to recognize them since not many are living Christ. Paul first wanted to gain Christ and then to be found in Christ by others. At the time Paul wrote the Epistle to the Philippians, he was in prison in Rome. He aspired to be found by his fellow prisoners and even by the household of Caesar (4:22) as a person in Christ.

KNOWING CHRIST IN EXPERIENCE

Verse 10 continues, "To know Him...." The excellency of the knowledge of Christ (v. 8) which Paul had was according to and by the revelation he received. Before he was saved, Paul was spiritually blind. He was zealous and desperate for the God whom his forefathers worshipped. However, on the way to Damascus, the Lord met him (Acts 9:1-9). At that time he received a direct revelation from the Lord (Gal. 1:15-16) concerning the wonderful Christ, the very embodiment of the God whom his forefathers worshipped. Paul's knowledge of Christ by revelation issued in the excellency of the knowledge of Christ. However, after receiving this excellent knowledge by revelation, he still sought a further knowledge, a knowledge not by revelation but by experience.

"To know" is an infinitive, indicating that the matters mentioned in the preceding verses are the qualifications for Paul to know Christ further experientially. These qualifications are: 1) counting the religious things which were gains loss on account of Christ; 2) counting also all things loss on account of the excellency of the knowledge of Christ; and 3) to be found in Christ, having the righteousness of God based upon faith. We may have the excellency of the knowledge of certain foods by looking at a menu, but we may never have tasted them. To taste the food requires certain qualifications. Paul was qualified to know Christ by being in the proper position and condition. He repudiated the things of traditional religion, including his former status in Judaism (Phil. 3:5-7). Moreover, he counted all things to be loss on account of Christ that he might gain Christ and be found in Him, not having his own righteousness which is of the law but the righteousness that is out of God. The Jews were found having the righteousness of the Mosaic law, but Paul lived in a condition of having the righteousness of God, which is God Himself in Christ as His embodiment. By being in such a condition, Paul was qualified to know Christ in experience.

KNOWING THE POWER OF HIS RESURRECTION

Verse 10 says, "To know Him and the power of His resurrection and the fellowship of His sufferings, being conformed to His death." When Paul wrote the Epistle to the Philippians, he had the experiential knowledge of Christ and was experiencing the power of His resurrection. While in the Roman prison, he may have been bound in stocks under the threat of execution by being beheaded or thrown to wild beasts in the amphitheater. In that situation he needed to know the power of the resurrection of Christ. The power of Christ's resurrection is His resurrection life which raised Him from among the dead (Eph. 1:19-20). It is the resurrected and resurrecting

Christ. This power was in Paul as the bountiful supply of the Spirit of Jesus Christ (Phil. 1:19). The reality of the power of Christ's resurrection is the Spirit (Rom. 8:11), and the bountiful supply of the Spirit is the power of resurrection. The nature of Christ's resurrection is the Spirit of Jesus Christ. Without the Spirit of Jesus Christ, there is no resurrection.

Today the Spirit is in our human spirit. The way to experientially know the power of resurrection is to turn to our spirit and remain in our spirit. It may not be necessary to pray to remain in our spirit. We may simply praise, sing hallelujahs, and shout triumphantly. This is the way to experience the power of Christ's resurrection.

In order to experience the power of resurrection, we are brought into suffering. Paul experienced the power of resurrection in a Roman prison. If we do not experience suffering, we cannot know this power. In this sense, the power of resurrection needs a "prison." Marriage life is an example of this kind of imprisonment. In a good sense, our marriage does not usher us into a banquet but into a "prison."

The cross of Christ may be compared to a cooking mold. When dough is pushed into shaped molds and cooked, the result is a bread or pastry in the shape of the mold. We are the "dough" that has been put into the "mold" of the cross by the power of resurrection. Our marriage life is a part of that mold. In one sense, marriage life is not an enjoying life; it is a suffering life. Paul said that those who marry will have affliction in the flesh (1 Cor. 7:28). However, marriage has been sovereignly ordained by the Lord. Unless one has received a special gift from the Lord (Matt. 19:10-12), he should not remain unmarried. Our children are also a part of the mold of the cross. I have seen many parents suffer because of their children.

To experientially know the power of Christ's resurrection needs us to be put into the mold of suffering. In Philippians 3:10 Paul speaks of the fellowship of Christ's sufferings. The Lord Jesus calls us to follow Him in His sufferings, bearing the cross (Matt. 16:24). To bear the cross is to enjoy the fellowship of the sufferings of the Lord Jesus.

BEING CONFORMED TO HIS DEATH

Philippians 3:10 first speaks of knowing Christ as a wonderful person. We can never exhaust telling who He is. Second, it speaks of knowing the power of His resurrection and the fellowship of His sufferings. Then while we are experientially enjoying the fellowship of His sufferings, we are being conformed to His death. The death of Christ is a mold. We are living in this mold of death. Christ's death should be the mold of our life. We will all eventually declare: "I am not only living; I am dying. I die to everything; I am a dying person. My living is in the mold of Christ's death."

We are not conformed to the death of Adam. The death of Adam is a terrible thing, but Christ's death is sweet. While we are living, we die in the mold of His death. We are enjoying knowing Christ experientially; we are enjoying knowing the power of Christ's resurrection; and we are enjoying knowing the fellowship of His sufferings. While we are in the enjoyment of this experiential knowledge, we are being conformed to the mold of His death.

Hymn #631 in *Hymns* says:

> If I'd know Christ's risen power,
>   I must ever love the Cross;
> Life from death alone arises;
>   There's no gain except by loss.

> If no death, no life,
>   If no death, no life;
> Life from death alone arises;
>   If no death, no life.

> If I'd have Christ formed within me,
>   I must breathe my final breath,
> Live within the Cross's shadow,
>   Put my soul-life e'er to death.

> If God thru th' Eternal Spirit
>   Nail me ever with the Lord;
> Only then as death is working
>   Will His life thru me be poured.

We are persons under the shadow of the cross of Christ. The Christian life is both a living life and a dying life. We live, but we live in the mold of the death of Christ. When the Lord Jesus lived on the earth, He was being crucified every day. Every day He lived a crucified life. We also can live such a life because we have the power of His resurrection. As we have seen, this power is the person of Christ, and Christ today is the Spirit of Jesus Christ who is in our spirit. As we remain in our spirit, we experience this power in the shadow of the death of Christ. Every day our spouse and children are the "shadows of death" to us. Our children may be very enjoyable to us at first. However, one day they may become shadows, and the more they grow, the darker the shadows may become. Eventually, our children will put us into the mold of the cross. We should simply remain there and say, "Hallelujah!"

Not only are our marriage life and family life the mold of the cross, but even the church life becomes the mold of the cross to us. Certain saints may wonder why there are hardships in the "glorious church life," and eventually the church life may not seem so glorious to them. Every brother and sister may seem to be a "dark shadow." This may cause some to consider moving to a new locality. However, they may discover that the church in the locality to which they move is even darker. Furthermore, if they leave the church, their situation will become darker still. We have no place to which we may escape. Every locality is a cross. This is our destiny. We have been destined to pass through the cross. Only when we are in the New Jerusalem in the new heavens and new earth will we be out of the shadow of death. In the New Jerusalem there will be no night and no shadow (Rev. 21:25). However, today there are shadows of the cross everywhere.

Praise the Lord that within us there is the power of resurrection. Paul said, "I can do all things in Him who empowers me" (Phil. 4:13). The One who empowers us is the power of resurrection. By Him we can live a life that expresses and magnifies Christ (Phil. 1:20).

THE EXPERIENCE AND GROWTH IN LIFE

MESSAGE THIRTEEN

THE EXPERIENCE OF LIFE

(7)

Scripture Reading: Phil. 1:19-21; 2:12-16; 3:9-10; 4:2-8, 12-13

Prayer: Lord, thank You for Your presence and Your rich anointing. Lord, we know that this is all that we need. Lord, we are still looking to You to show us Your way of life. Show us how You would like for us to go on in this way. Open up Your Word to us, and give us the depths of the mysteries concerning Yourself being life to us. Amen.

SALVATION BEING TO MAGNIFY CHRIST

Philippians 1:19-21 says, "For I know that for me this shall turn out to salvation through your petition and the bountiful supply of the Spirit of Jesus Christ, according to my earnest expectation and hope that in nothing I shall be put to shame, but with all boldness, as always, even now Christ shall be magnified in my body, whether through life or through death; for to me to live is Christ, and to die is gain." The main thought in these verses is salvation. To Paul salvation was to magnify Christ even under persecution and imprisonment. If Paul failed to magnify Christ, that would be a shame to him; but if he magnified Christ, this would be his salvation. Salvation to Paul was to magnify Christ regardless of the circumstances.

Salvation (in ch. 1 Philippians) = To be saved from not magnifying Christ.

SALVATION FROM MURMURINGS AND REASONINGS

In chapter one sufferings turn out to salvation, but in chapter two we have to carry out our salvation. Philippians 2:12-16 says, "So then, my beloved, even as you have always obeyed, not only as in my presence, but now much rather in my absence, work out your own salvation with fear and trembling; for it is God who operates in you both the willing and the working for His good pleasure. Do all things without murmurings and reasonings, that you may become blameless and guileless, children of God without blemish in the midst of a crooked and perverted generation, among whom you shine as lights in the world, holding forth the word of life, for my boasting in the day of Christ, that I have not run in vain nor labored in vain."

Salvation in chapter two is **from murmurings and reasonings**. The sisters murmur and the brothers reason. Murmurings and reasonings are two small enemies to the experience of Christ. Because they seem to be so small, we often do not care about them, but they are two signs which indicate that we have been defeated in living Christ. No one who lives Christ murmurs or reasons. Murmurings and reasonings kill our life of living Christ. We should carry out a life without murmurings and reasonings. Between husbands and wives, fathers and mothers, brothers and sisters, there are a lot of murmurings and reasonings. The females mostly murmur, and the males mostly reason. Even in the so-called "glorious church life," these things exist. Because we murmur and reason, we fail in carrying out our salvation.

Salvation in chapter two has many elements. Doing things without murmurings and doing things without reasonings are two elements of salvation which we have to work out. Other elements of this salvation are included in verse 15, which says, "That you may become blameless and guileless, children of God without blemish in the midst of a crooked and perverted generation." In order to be blameless and guileless children of God without blemish in the midst of a crooked and perverted generation, we must be saved from murmurings and reasonings. The word "perverted" in this verse means to be warped or twisted. Today's perverted generation is warped and twisted. In such a generation we as children of God, having God's life and nature, "shine as lights in the world, holding forth the word of life" (vv. 15-16).

We have to shine as luminaries. A luminary is an object which shines with no light of its own; it shines by reflecting light. Christ is the true light (John 1:9; 8:12) typified by the light of the sun. We as luminaries reflect this light into the world. To "shine as lights" is equal to "holding forth the word of life." To hold forth in Greek means to apply, to present, to offer. We should always have something of Christ to present, to offer, to the people of the world. To hold forth Christ is to shine. To only speak is inadequate; we have to shine. This shining depends upon what we are, not upon our speaking. We must be people who shine by reflecting Christ as the light.

Salvation comprises several elements in chapter two: not murmuring, not reasoning, becoming blameless and guileless children of God in the midst of a crooked, perverted, warped, and twisted generation, shining as luminaries to reflect Christ, and holding forth the word of life. This salvation with all of these elements is the salvation which we should carry out.

SALVATION BEING THE RIGHTEOUSNESS OF GOD

In Philippians 3:9-10 Paul desired to "be found in Him, not having my own righteousness which is of the law, but that which is through the faith of Christ, the righteousness which is of God based on faith, to know Him and the power of His resurrection and the fellowship of His sufferings, being conformed to His death." To be found in Christ, having the righteousness which is of God based upon faith, is to have God Himself embodied in Christ as righteousness. The Christ we live out in chapter one is our righteousness in chapter three. The righteousness of God based upon faith in chapter three is the Christ we must live and magnify in chapter one. When we live and magnify Christ according to chapter one, people will find us in Christ, not having our own natural goodness or natural virtues, but having Christ as our righteousness.

When we see this vision of the experience of life and look at our present situation, we have to admit that we are far off from this experience. We may study the Bible and pray much, but we are still very much in ourselves and not very much in Christ. We are usually in ourselves, having only our good behavior. One brother's characteristic may be his slowness, while another brother's characteristic may be his quickness. When I contact such brothers, I may find them only partially in Christ and mainly in their peculiar characteristics. But the Apostle Paul's particular characteristic was the righteousness of God, the Christ he lived and magnified. In Philippians 1 Paul expected and earnestly hoped to live and magnify Christ. Then in chapter three he desired to be found in the very Christ he lived and magnified. Being found in Christ, he would have no goodness of himself, but the righteousness of God, who is Christ as the embodiment of God.

Each chapter of Philippians presents a particular aspect of this salvation. We experience Christ as our salvation in aspect after aspect. Salvation has a long-term aspect and a short-term aspect. Chapter one deals with salvation in its life-long or long-term aspect, and chapter two deals with salvation in its daily or short-term aspect. These are two aspects of the same salvation. Eventually, this salvation also has the aspect of being the righteousness of God as seen in chapter three.

In the book of Philippians, Paul speaks in a very practical way concerning God's salvation, covering its lifelong aspect, its daily aspect, and its aspect of being the righteousness of God. This last aspect includes Christ as God's embodiment lived out and magnified by us. The righteousness of God in chapter three equals the salvation mentioned in the two preceding chapters. In its daily aspect small things such as murmurings and reasonings are mentioned because daily life among people on this earth is mainly a matter of murmurings and reasonings.

THINKING THE SAME THING

In Philippians 4:2 Paul said that he besought Euodias and Syntyche to think the same thing in the Lord. In living Christ, the hardest thing to do is to think the same thing. To enjoy Christ may seem to be easy, but without the real enjoyment of Christ, we all would be dissenting, not thinking the same thing. We would be dissenting not only toward the elders but also toward everyone else. We would be agreeable only with ourselves. When we come to serve by arranging the chairs, we may arrange the chairs and murmur at the same time because the way the chairs are arranged and cleaned may not suit us. Because our fallen nature is full of dissension, it is difficult to see real harmony not only in our family life but also in the church life. Harmony in the church life is a real treasure.

In the experience of enjoying Christ, living Christ, and magnifying Christ, there are many obstacles. The first obstacle is murmurings and reasonings. The second obstacle is dissension. Paul was a very skillful writer. When he wrote about these two good sisters, he said, "I beseech Euodias, and I beseech Syntyche, to think the same thing in the Lord. Yes, I ask you also, genuine yokefellow, assist them, who contended with me in the gospel, with both Clement and the rest of my fellow workers, whose names are in the book of life" (Phil. 4:2-3). Paul first touched the negative problem of dissension between two of his fellow workers, exhorting them to think the same thing. He then highly appraised them for the positive point of their service in the gospel. Then as a conclusion, he led them to rejoice (v. 4).

TAKING CHRIST AS OUR FORBEARANCE

Philippians 4:5 says, "Let your forbearance be known to all men." This means that you should be found in forbearance by all the saints. The word *forbearance* is difficult to explain completely. Many may define forbearance as patience or long-suffering. However, forbearance is more than patience or long-suffering. It is reasonableness, considerateness, and consideration in dealing with others, without strictness of legal right. First, if we would be forbearing, we must be reasonable and fair. We must do things in a reasonable and fair way. Second, we have to consider others. To be forbearing is to consider how others will be affected by what we do or say. We should consider whether or not our words would damage people. We have to be very considerate in dealing with others, avoiding strictness.

The Chinese translation of Philippians uses a word for forbearance which means to fit in with another's situation. When we lack forbearance, we are unable to fit in with another's situation. Brothers or sisters may be living together in an apartment in a very pleasant way. When another brother or sister comes in who lacks forbearance, trouble may be stirred up, destroying the peaceful situation. But when a brother or sister who is full of forbearance comes into a situation in which brothers or sisters are having problems, he or she becomes a peacemaker. Whatever that brother or sister says or does keeps everyone comfortable. Everyone is calmed down, and everyone feels that everything is all right in the apartment.

Although every verse of Philippians 4 mentions a new item concerning the experience of Christ, all of these items are related to one another. A proper Christian life of living and magnifying Christ will not dissent with others, will always rejoice, will always forbear, and will have no anxiety (v. 6). This kind of life enjoys the peace of God (v. 7).

THE EXPRESSION OF THE LIFE
THAT LIVES CHRIST

In Philippians 4:8 Paul presents six items which express the life that lives Christ. This verse says, "For the rest, brothers, whatever is true, whatever is honorable, whatever is righteous, whatever is pure, whatever is lovely, whatever is well-spoken of...." These items form three pairs. The first pair is true and honorable. The second pair is righteous and pure. The third pair is lovely and well-spoken of. Verse 8 concludes with two matters: "If there is any virtue and if any praise, take account of these things." All of these items are very human. Some saints are very desirous to live Christ but in a way that is not very human. These six items with two concluding matters describe how human we should be in living Christ. We should be true, without any pretense or falsehood. We also should be honorable, which means that we are people who invite honor, regard, and respect from others. As those who live Christ, we should be righteous before God and men, and we should also be pure. To be righteous is to be right without; to be pure is to be single in our intention and motive within. We must be right without and pure within. We should also be lovely and well-spoken of. To be lovely is to be lovable, agreeable, and endearing. To be well-spoken of is to be of good repute, renowned, attractive, winning, gracious, and even charming.

Although all of the foregoing items are human virtues, we must realize that these human virtues are the vessel created by God to contain His attributes. A glove is made in the image and likeness of a hand as a container for the hand with its fingers. Without the hand with its fingers, the glove is empty. In the same way, we were made in God's image and likeness. He is the true God, and He has made us in a way that we can contain Him. God is true, and man can also be true. God is honorable, and God also made man with honor. The items in Philippians 4:8 are not only the virtues of man, but also the attributes of God.

We are vessels made to contain God for His expression, so we have the outward form of these attributes but not their reality. When we live Christ, who is the embodiment of God with all the attributes of God, He fills up all of our empty virtues. God's attributes then become our virtues. Thus, living Christ makes us very human. We should not only be spiritual and heavenly but also be true, honorable, righteous, pure, lovely, and well-spoken of. These human virtues with the divine attributes are the detailed expression of the Christ we live and magnify. If we are not lovely and honorable, we are not expressing Christ. If we do not live an honorable life, we are not living Christ. If we live and magnify Christ, we will surely live an honorable life.

THE WAY TO LIVE CHRIST

The way for us to live Christ with all of these human virtues with the divine attributes is found in verse 13, which says, "I can do all things in Him who empowers me." We can be true, honorable, righteous, pure, lovely, and well-spoken of in Christ, the One who empowers us. In Christ, the One we live, we can do all things.

TAKING CHRIST AS OUR SECRET

The Christ we live is not only our power but also our secret. Philippians 4:12 says, "I know both how to be abased, and I know how to abound; in everything and in all things I have learned the secret both to be filled and to hunger, both to abound and to be in want." "To abound" is to be rich, and "to be abased" is to be poor. Paul knew how to handle both poverty and abundance. Poverty would not defeat him, and riches would not spoil him. "To be filled" means to be rich with more than enough to eat, and "to hunger" means to be poor, to lack, to suffer privation with not enough to eat. Paul had learned the secret both of being rich and of being poor.

The book of Philippians ends with a life not dissenting with others, full of forbearance, without anxiety, and full of human virtues. Philippians ends with a person who is so true, honorable, righteous, pure, lovely, and well-spoken of. Such a person is full of human virtues with the divine attributes as their contents to express Christ in a human way. We also should be such persons. The secret of such a life is Christ, the One who empowers us. To live and magnify Christ, having the righteousness of God based upon faith, is our salvation.

THE EXPERIENCE AND GROWTH IN LIFE

MESSAGE FOURTEEN

THE GROWTH IN LIFE

(7)

Scripture Reading: Phil. 4:2-8

Philippians 1 speaks of salvation through the bountiful supply of the Spirit of Jesus Christ (v. 19), living Christ (v. 21), and magnifying Christ (v. 20). In chapter two salvation is spoken of again. Verse 12 says, "Work out your own salvation with fear and trembling." Verse 15 says that we shine as lights in the world. We are luminaries reflecting Christ as light. This shining is the holding forth, the applying, presenting, and offering of the word of life (v. 16). Philippians 3 speaks of the righteousness of God based on faith (v. 9). Righteousness in chapter three equals the salvation in chapters one and two. Chapter three also speaks of our goal (v. 14) and our pursuing (v. 12).

THINKING THE SAME THING
AND REJOICING IN THE LORD

The first matter spoken of in Philippians 4 is thinking the same thing. Verse 2 says, "I beseech Euodias, and I beseech Syntyche, to think the same thing in the Lord." According to our dissenting nature, we often cannot agree with others. If someone suggests that we do one thing, we may propose to do the opposite instead. Before a young child knows many other words, he can already say "No!" to his mother. From our youth we have learned to say no to everyone else and yes to ourselves. This is dissenting, and dissenting is rebellion.

The desire for prestige and respect is at the root of our dissenting. Even if we are wrong about something, we may still try to claim our dignity in that situation. We can observe this fallen, human behavior everywhere. Many of the arguments ꞵetween children in a family center around the issue of prestige. The desire for prestige and the dissenting it produces are of the self.

Verse 4 says, "Rejoice in the Lord always; again I will say, rejoice." If we think the same thing and are not dissenting, we can rejoice. According to human experience, a dissenting person is rarely joyful. Rather, those who are dissenting are full of complaints, murmurings, and reasonings (2:14). Philippians 4:5 says, "Let your forbearance be known to all men." Forbearance is reasonableness, considerateness, and consideration in dealing with others, without strictness of legal right. Those who are forbearing can readily agree with and follow others. However, if we are dissenting persons, we will not be able to forbear with others. As a result we will have anxiety (v. 6). The way to be at peace and be released from anxiety is to be forbearing with everyone.

CHRIST AS THE REALITY OF OUR HUMAN VIRTUES

Verse 8 says, "For the rest, brothers, whatever is true, whatever is honorable, whatever is righteous, whatever is pure, whatever is lovely, whatever is well-spoken of, if there is any virtue and if any praise, take account of these things." The items listed in this verse are the virtues of a proper humanity. When we are not dissenting, we can rejoice and have forbearance. As those who forbear with others, we will live a life that is truthful, honorable, venerable, right, pure, and single, with no mixture in our motive. Then our living will be lovely and well-spoken of. As a result, we will have virtues and things worthy of praise. This is the proper living of a proper human being.

All the items spoken of in Philippians 1 through 3 are the elements of the proper human living in chapter four. To live Christ in chapter one is to live a life that is true, honorable, right, pure, lovely, and well-spoken of, full of virtues and praise. Likewise, as luminaries reflecting Christ in chapter two, our expression is a life that is pure, right, honorable, and true. The way to live such a life is to live Christ. However, many unbelievers endeavor in themselves to have these human virtues. They are like a glove without a hand in it.

Their virtues are empty and without reality. When we live Christ, we have the reality of all the human virtues, including truthfulness, honor, righteousness, and purity.

When some new believers begin to seek the Lord, they may desire to be like the angels. What we need to be, however, are proper human beings. A proper human being is a person filled with Christ as the reality of his human virtues. Christ must be our truthfulness, honor, righteousness, purity, and every item of our human virtues. To be a proper human being in this way is to express God through His divine attributes in our human virtues, to have a human life filled with Christ as the reality of the attributes of God. A proper person is full of virtues, and Christ as the embodiment of God is the content, the reality, of his virtues.

To be a person full of Christ as the proper virtues is to experience God's salvation. In Philippians 1 salvation is to live Christ and magnify Christ in any circumstance. Chapter two shows us that this salvation is to reflect Christ by holding forth the word of life. In chapter three salvation is the righteousness of God, who is God Himself embodied in Christ. Then in chapter four, there is the life that is true, honorable, righteous, pure, lovely, well-spoken of, and full of virtue and praise.

The reality of such a life is Christ. Therefore, all four chapters of Philippians refer to the all-inclusive, living person of Christ. In chapter one Christ is our long-term salvation, in chapter two Christ is our daily salvation, and in chapter three Christ is the righteousness of God. Then in chapter four Christ is all the virtues of our humanity.

CHRIST AS OUR DAILY VIRTUES

We must build up a proper daily life with a proper character. To merely behave in a certain way is a performance and is hypocrisy. Our living should not be a performance. Rather, we should be proper persons with a proper living. "To live Christ" is not merely a slogan. The living of Christ must be the reality of our daily life. The revelations in Philippians 1 through 3 concerning the salvation and righteousness of God are very high. However, they all point to the living of Christ as the

..ivine reality in our human virtues. Therefore, in chapter four Paul applied these revelations to our practical daily life. In verse 2 he said, "I beseech Euodias, and I beseech Syntyche, to think the same thing in the Lord." According to verse 3, these were very good sisters who had been helpful to Paul. These sisters were living Christ and magnifying Christ to a certain extent. However, they were still dissenting. Spiritually speaking, they were appraised highly. Their names are in the book of life, and they labored with Paul and Clement (v. 3), but in their practical life there was a big problem. In the same way, we may speak of spiritual things, but our person may not be true, honorable, righteous, pure, and lovely.

One aspect of our daily life is the way we dress. We should learn to dress properly at all times. To dress properly only when we know someone is coming to visit us is hypocrisy. It is not a genuine daily life. If we are loose in the matter of dress, we are probably loose in everything else as well. In the same way, if we do not make our bed after rising in the morning, it is not likely that we can study the Bible very well.

The very Christ whom we live and preach must be our daily virtues. Our love for people should not merely be human love, but human love filled with and expressing the divine love, which is Christ, the embodiment of the processed Triune God. The ethical philosophers of China stressed the development of the human virtues. They taught that we need to develop the sense of our conscience, which they called the "bright virtue." If some would go to China to teach them of Christ as the divine love filling our love, the Chinese scholars could be subdued. We not only have a conscience; we also have the embodiment of the processed Triune God, who today is the Spirit of Jesus Christ, the all-inclusive, consummated, sevenfold intensified Spirit. Such a Christ is our motivator, the inward motivating power. Christ as our motivating power may be compared to an electric motor empowering the development of our human virtues.

In Philippians 1 the motivator is the Spirit of Jesus Christ (v. 19) who is the bountiful, all-inclusive, all-capable, and all-sufficient supply. Christ passed through incarnation, death, resurrection, ascension, and enthronement by the all-inclusive Spirit. Now this Spirit, who is the consummation of the Triune God, is in our human spirit. In chapter two the motivator is the inner-operating God (v. 13), the processed Triune God embodied in Christ who became a life-giving Spirit (1 Cor. 15:45b). In chapter three the motivator is the power of Christ's resurrection, and this power is also the processed Triune God as the all-inclusive Spirit of Jesus Christ. The Spirit of Jesus Christ, the inner-operating God, and the power of His resurrection refer to the same person.

The motivator in chapter four is seen in verse 13, which says, "I can do all things in Him who empowers me." This motivator is the Spirit of Jesus Christ, the operating God, and the consummated Triune God as the power of resurrection. He is not only in us, but we are also in Him. In this One who empowers and strengthens us, we can do all things. "All things" refers to every aspect of our human virtue, as spoken of in chapters one through four. We can be true, honorable, right, pure, lovely, and well-spoken of in Him. We can live the top human life, full of human virtues filled with the divine attributes.

QUESTIONS AND ANSWERS

Question: How do we reconcile the high teachings in Philippians 1 through 3 with the emphasis on the details of our daily life in chapter four?

Answer: Living Christ and our daily life do not need to be reconciled; they are one. The very Christ whom we live and magnify in Philippians 1 should be our virtues in our daily life in Philippians 4. The reality of all the items of our virtues, such as truthfulness, honor, righteousness, and purity, is Christ, who is the righteousness of God based on faith.

Question: How can attention to the details in our daily life help us?

Answer: Attention to details will help us to go to Christ. We have to have a morning watch to meet the Lord Jesus, to enjoy and contact Him. We need to have the assurance that through the cleansing of His blood we have the anointing. The anointing is Christ moving in us, and the moving of Christ is His presence. Early in the morning, regardless of how busy we are, we must have at least some time to stay in the presence of the Lord. Then we will meet Him, and He will supply us. He will become the motivator and the "motor" for our Christian life. Then, if we are wrong in some aspect of our daily life, He will bother us within. In this way, we will learn how to live Christ.

THE EXPERIENCE AND GROWTH IN LIFE

MESSAGE FIFTEEN

THE EXPERIENCE OF LIFE

(8)

Scripture Reading: Phil. 4:5-8

LETTING OUR REQUESTS BE MADE KNOWN TO GOD

Philippians 4:5-6 says, "Let your forbearance be known to all men. The Lord is near. In nothing be anxious, but in everything, by prayer and petition with thanksgiving, let your requests be made known to God." Prayer is general with the essence of worship and fellowship; petition is special for particular needs. Both our prayer and petition should be accompanied by thanksgiving to the Lord. The English preposition *to* in the phrase "to God" is the Greek preposition *pros*. This preposition is often translated "with" (John 1:1; Mark 9:19; Matt. 26:55; 2 Cor. 5:8; 1 Cor. 16:6; 1 John 1:2). It denotes motion towards, in the sense of a living union and communion; thus, it implies fellowship. Hence, the meaning of "to God" here is in fellowship with God. John 1:1 uses the preposition *pros* in the phrase "the Word was with *(pros)* God." Such a word conveys the thought of traffic, something going back and forth. It denotes motion toward some object which produces a transaction in the sense of a living union. Based upon this union, there is communion which is a communication or fellowship.

Whenever we pray, making our petition in the proper way, there should be some traffic between us and God. Something from us should move toward God, causing God to respond to us. This moving back and forth is fellowship. This is the proper meaning of the word *fellowship*. Fellowship is actually the dispensing of God for man to receive. The fellowship we have with God, on God's side, is His dispensing, and, on our side, our receiving. He dispenses, and we receive. The more fellowship we have, the more we receive of God through His dispensing.

When we are short of something, we may become anxious. We should not bear this anxiety by ourselves. We should let God know, by making our requests to Him, by prayer and petition with thanksgiving. This is the kind of prayer we should have. We do not need to pray in the way of begging God to do things for us. We should just tell Him what we need, that is, we should let Him know, not keeping anything within ourselves. If we have any worry or anxiety, we should just tell Him. Our letting Him know is our motion toward Him. Then His response is His dispensing, His mingling of Himself with us, even before He answers our request. This mingling of divinity with humanity is the mingling of two entities, the divine entity and the human entity.

Philippians 4:6 is apparently a very simple verse since it exhorts us not to worry and to let God know our requests. However, the reality this word reveals is not so simple or shallow. Electricity also is apparently very simple. If you need heat or light you just push a button, and you get heat or light. If you want cold air, you just push another button. The application of electricity is very simple, but the science of electricity is not so simple. If electricity were dispensed into you without limit, you would die of its electrical current. The higher the current of electricity is, the quicker you would die. But with the "divine electricity," the divine dispensing, the more God you receive, the more you live. On the one hand, as you receive this divine electricity, the old man dies, but on the other hand, the new man lives. The divine dispensing is also a science, and the study of the divine dispensing can never be exhausted.

FORBEARANCE BEING THE SUM TOTAL OF THE HUMAN VIRTUES

Philippians 4:5-8 form one section in which the first item touched is forbearance. The content of forbearance includes all the human virtues mentioned in verse 8. Forbearance is the sum total of our human virtues. Forbearance is the top virtue because it is all-inclusive. Eventually, forbearance is just Christ Himself.

In verse 5 we are encouraged to express Christ as our forbearance. But the thing which opposes forbearance is our anxiety (v. 6). Anxiety is versus forbearance. If you live Christ, the character of your expression will be forbearance. But if you are a person who is full of anxiety, the character of your expression will be worry. Our anxiety can be turned into forbearance by bringing every need, every request, to God (v. 6) and by conversing with Him. To converse implies a kind of traffic back and forth. Every morning, regardless of how busy we are, we need such traffic between us and God. This kind of traffic brings in the divine dispensing, reduces our anxiety, and builds up our forbearance. It is by this traffic, the fellowship between us and God, that we enjoy the divine dispensing.

When you are full of forbearance, it will be difficult for you to lose your temper or to condemn or criticize others. You also will not appraise people too highly. You will be fitting in every way. As a guest in someone's home, you may be served tea. If you are a person full of forbearance, whether the tea is hot, cold, or lukewarm, you will not express anything. It should also be the same in the church life. If you are a person full of forbearance, the church life may be full of turmoil, but to your feeling of forbearance, the church life is wonderful. This feeling may seem contrary to the facts, but according to your sense of forbearance, the church is really wonderful. The church is always wonderful according to its nature, but sometimes according to its condition, it may not be so wonderful. Regardless of its condition, we should always go along with the church according to its nature. Your father is your father by birth, not by his condition. At times his condition may not be so good, but he is still your father.

Forbearance is to be very moderate and very natural, neither too hot nor too cold. With forbearance we are able to go along with any person, regardless of their temperament or disposition. If, however, we move and act only according to our own likes and dislikes, we do not have a life of forbearance. When we have learned the lessons in the divine life, we can easily be with another person in their situation without any complaints. If they walk fast, we will walk fast. If they walk slowly, we will walk slowly. If they stop, we will stop. If they sit down, we will sit down. Forbearance is a real test to the kind of life we are living. Many times, for example, the wife cannot sit in the car while her husband is driving without complaining about his driving. It is very difficult for the wife to forbear while her husband drives.

WHATEVER IS HONORABLE

A virtue mentioned in Philippians 4:8 is "honorable." Honor means dignity. With God in His divinity, it is a matter of His glory, but with us in our humanity, it is a matter of honor or dignity. When Christ ascended to the heavens, He was crowned with both glory and honor (Heb. 2:7) because He is a person who is both divine and human. In His divinity He received glory, and in His humanity He received honor and dignity.

VIRTUE AND PRAISE

Philippians 4:8 ends with the two matters of virtue and praise. Virtue is toward us, and praise is toward God. The eight items mentioned in verse 8 are divided into two categories. The first six items are categorized as "whatever is"; the last two, virtue and praise, are categorized as "if any." This indicates that the last two are a summing up of the six foregoing items, in all of which are some virtue or excellence and something worthy of praise. The first six items of truthfulness, honor, rightness, purity, loveliness, and being well-spoken of are human virtues summed up by the phrase "if there is any virtue." "If any praise" sums up the entire verse including all the foregoing items. "Praise" refers to the expression of God. Praise means that God is expressed to such an extent that others praise God. The expression of God causes others to praise God. Virtue and praise indicate that humanity with its virtues expresses God. These seven items in Philippians 4:8 eventually consummate in praise.

In writing these words, the Apostle Paul must have had a great deal of consideration. Out of hundreds of human virtues, Paul selected only six. Then as a conclusion, he used only the two items of virtue and praise. Virtue sums up the six fore-going items, and praise concludes the entire section. When our human virtues express God's divine attributes, praise is offered to God. This is exactly the same thought as that in Matthew 5:16. When others see our good works (human virtues), they glorify (praise) our Father who is in the heavens. The Christian life is a life which always expresses God in human virtues. As a result, such a life always brings glory and praise to God.

The way to live a life which is full of virtues expressing God and bringing glory and praise to God is in Christ, the One who empowers us (Phil. 4:13). The Chinese ethical scholars taught concerning the development of human virtues. But the development of human virtues taught by them could never produce any glory and praise to God. When we love and honor our parents, our love and honor must be different from the human honor taught by the Chinese ethical scholars. Their honor does not have the taste or flavor of anything divine. Our honor to our parents should be full of humanity, and it should also have the flavor of divinity within it. This flavor and taste of God is the difference between the unbeliever's honor and the believer's honor. The Christian's honor has the smell and flavor of the divine attributes. In our experience, quite often our honor seems to lack this quality of divinity. This is because we fail to live Christ. If we do not live Christ, we may still honor our parents, but this honor will have no divine flavor. Therefore, we need to grow in the divine life and live Christ. Then the honor toward our parents will have the divine flavor.

When the Western missionaries went to China, the Chinese scholars asked why they should become Christians when their own teaching concerning honor was stronger than the teaching of honor in the Bible. Many of the missionaries may not have known what or how to answer them. Today, however, we have the answer. Regardless of how high the Chinese ethical teaching of honor may be, it still does not have anything divine in it. Though the Christian honor may seem to be a little lower than that of the Chinese scholars, in reality, the proper Christian honor is much higher because it has the divine flavor.

In the societies of the Western world, the matter of loving our neighbor is highly appreciated. Even atheists may talk about loving others. Some wealthy men have given their wealth to hospitals or other charitable causes. They may love others by donating their wealth to hospitals or schools, but there is no flavor of God in their giving. Rather, the flavor is one of vainglory. This is because whoever donated the money for the hospital may receive some recognition of his donation by a memorial stone commemorating his gift. This kind of love is void of the flavor and taste of God. Yet a brother who does not have much money may show his love by giving a needy saint most of his savings without anyone's knowledge. This kind of love bears the flavor of God, and it is different from mere human love. The difference is in the nature and source of the love. To have the love which has the flavor of God depends upon the person who does it, not on what you do. If you do it in yourself, there is no flavor of God. But if you do it through God and God does it through you, there is much flavor of God.

Philippians 4:8 begins with truthfulness and ends with praise. The Christian life is a life full of human virtues which produce glory and praise to God. Verses 5 through 8 show us that the proper Christian life is a life of the mingling of divinity with humanity.

MAN BEING IN GOD'S IMAGE TO EXPRESS THE DIVINE ATTRIBUTES OF LOVE, LIGHT, HOLINESS, AND RIGHTEOUSNESS

Genesis 1:26 is one of the most significant verses in the entire Bible, especially in the Old Testament. After God created the heavens and the earth, He said, "Let us make man in our image, after our likeness." "Let us" indicates that there was a conversation among the divine Trinity—the Father, Son, and Spirit—concerning the creation of man. This verse conveys a great mystery. The booklet *The Mystery of Human Life* stresses the mystery in Genesis 1:26 very much. The mystery of human life is that man is made in the image of God and according to His likeness. Image denotes what God is, and likeness denotes a kind of form.

Man was made in the image of what God is. God in His nature is Spirit (John 4:24), whereas God in His image is love, light, holiness, and righteousness. A gold ring in nature is gold, but in its image it is a ring. God being Spirit refers to His nature, and God being love, light, holiness, and righteousness refers to His image.

In the Old Testament, the Ten Commandments are a portrait of what God is, a portrait of the One who gave the law. The laws used in most of human society today are based upon Roman law. Roman law is primarily based upon the Ten Commandments. The elements which constitute the Ten Commandments are love, light, holiness, and righteousness. These four elements are the attributes of God's image. God in His image is love, light, holiness, and righteousness. Therefore, when God made man in His image, God made man in love, in light, in holiness, and in righteousness. Human beings, whether Christians or non-Christians, have the character of love, light, holiness, and righteousness. No one likes to be dark; everyone likes to be in the light. No one likes to be so common; everyone likes to be different or unique. No one likes to be wrong; everyone likes to be right. Animals do not have this kind of character, but we human beings do.

Through Adam's fall, these items of our human character were spoiled by the evil one when he entered into us. Because of this, there is often a battle within us. On the one hand, we love our parents, but when we lose our temper, we may become angry with them. This is the battle. We like to be honest, but often, when certain circumstances are present, we may lie. Though at times we win the battle, often we are not strong enough in our fallen nature to stand against the negative elements. In Romans 7:19-20 Paul said, "The good which I will, I do not; but the evil I do not will, this I practice. But if what I do not will, this I do, it is no longer I that do it but sin that dwells in me." Sin is personified, taking action like a person within us.

Through God's salvation we were put into God, and God also entered into us. Now within us there is a mingling of divinity with humanity. A glove with a hand as its content is one with the hand. The hand and the glove have become one

entity. The hand is inside of the glove, and the glove is outside of the hand. The glove expresses the hand, and the hand
strengthens and empowers the glove, making the glove so
real. This is the Christian life. As Christians we must remember that we are complicated people. We are people who have
been mingled with the divine Person, making us one spirit
with the Lord (1 Cor. 6:17). Although it is true to say that
Christ is our content and we are His expression, our relationship with Christ is even deeper and higher than this. We have
been mingled together with Christ. This is like grafting, in
which a branch of one tree grows and lives together with
another tree (Rom. 11:24).

The Christian life is the mingling of divinity with humanity. When we love, we must love by our love with God's love as
its content and reality. Apparently, it is only human love;
actually, it is the divine love. It is not only the divine love as
the content with the human love as its appearance, but also
the divine love mingled with the human love so that these two
loves become one love. Thus, it is hard to say whether it is the
human love or the divine love. In Philippians 4:8 the human
love is contained in the six items of truthfulness, honor, rightness, purity, loveliness, and being well-spoken of, and the
divine love is expressed in the last item, praise.

The practical mingling of divinity with humanity is carried
out by the traffic described in verse 6. We must come to God by
prayer often. This is the reason the New Testament tells us to
pray unceasingly (1 Thes. 5:17). To pray is to breathe God in. To
pray is also to have a traffic between us and God. This two-way
traffic is our union, communion, and fellowship. The current of
electricity is its traffic, communion, or fellowship. Without the
current of electricity, we could not enjoy the operation of electrical appliances such as lights. It is the same between us and
God. Within us there must always be traffic, a current, between
us and God. When we stop praying, the traffic stops. Then
whatever we do is something in ourselves without God. When
we pray unceasingly, keeping ourselves in the current, the
fellowship, the communion, the traffic, we enjoy the mingling
of divinity with humanity. Then as we exercise our love, we
express God's love. Our love is our virtue mingled with God's

love, God's attribute. We then become a mingled entity, a God-man, having divinity mingled with our humanity.

THE EXPERIENCE AND GROWTH IN LIFE

MESSAGE SIXTEEN

THE GROWTH IN LIFE

(8)

Scripture Reading: Rom. 5:10-11; 6:4-5; 8:2, 10, 6, 11, 13

RECONCILED THROUGH THE DEATH OF GOD'S SON, SAVED IN HIS LIFE, AND BOASTING IN GOD

Romans 5:10-11 says, "For if, while we were enemies, we were reconciled to God through the death of His Son, much more, having been reconciled, we shall be saved in His life. And not only so, but we also are boasting in God through our Lord Jesus Christ, through whom we have now received the reconciliation." Verse 10 speaks of the death of Christ and the life of Christ. We were reconciled to God through the death of Christ, and now we are being saved in the life of Christ.

According to verse 11, we also are boasting in God. Boast has the meaning of exult and glory. We are boasting, exulting, and glorying in God because we are being saved in His life. To exult is to be crazily happy. While we are being saved in the life of Christ, we should not be too quiet. Every day we have to boast, exult, and glory. This should be the expression of our salvation in the life of Christ.

We were reconciled to God through the death of Christ, and we are now being saved in His life. This salvation is not our eternal salvation but our daily, moment by moment salvation. If the trials that we undergo seem to last a long time, this may indicate that we are not enjoying our moment by moment salvation. If we are experiencing this salvation, we will boast and exult, and the trials will pass by quickly. By the Lord's sovereignty, we are often placed in trying situations. The way to enjoy this salvation in these situations is to boast, exult, and glory in God.

Paul's writing in Romans 5:10-11 was very careful. Moreover, he did not compose these verses merely according to doctrine but according to his experience. He did not say that we boast, exult, and glory in our salvation, but in the person of God. We are enjoying our salvation in God. This indicates that we have a direct contact, union, and connection with God. Our enjoyment in God may be compared to the enjoyment of a child with his mother. Little children care mainly for their mother's presence. The younger a child is, the closer he stays to his mother. You can take away many things from a baby without disturbing him, but you cannot take away the presence of his mother. In the same way, we enjoy the salvation of Christ in the person of God.

Paul's wording in these verses is wonderful, especially in his use of prepositions. It is through the death of God's Son that we are reconciled to God, but it is in His life that we are saved daily. This means that if we are not in God experientially, we cannot be saved in the life of Christ. We must have a direct, instant union with God. To be saved minute by minute, we must be in God, in the direct, constant, and instant union with God. Furthermore, we are now boasting, exulting, and glorying, not in the death of Christ or even in His life but in the person of the Triune God. We are one with Him, minute by minute.

WALKING IN NEWNESS OF LIFE AND
BEING IN THE LIKENESS OF HIS RESURRECTION

Romans 6 and 8 are an explanation of what it is to be saved in the life of Christ minute by minute. Romans 6:4-5 says, "We have been buried therefore with Him through baptism into death that as Christ was raised from among the dead through the glory of the Father, even so we also should walk in newness of life. For if we have grown together with Him in the likeness of His death, we shall be also in the likeness of His resurrection." Being saved in the life of Christ in Romans 5:10 corresponds with walking in newness of life in 6:4. If we are being saved in His life, then we are walking in newness of life. Sometimes a husband may give his wife an unpleasant look. In this situation the sister should simply walk in newness of life. This is to be saved in the life of Christ. However, if she returns the unpleasant look, she is not walking in the newness of Christ's life. Rather, she is in the oldness of Adam's death.

The newness of life in verse 4 equals resurrection in verse 5. When the Lord Jesus came out of the tomb, He had the newness of life. Resurrection is the newness of life, but death is oldness. With a dead person there is nothing but oldness, but in a resurrected person, there is newness of life. When a husband gives an unpleasant look to his wife, the wife should return an exulting face. Such a face is a face in the likeness of resurrection. Our salvation in our daily life is a walk in newness of life, and to walk in newness of life is to live a life in resurrection.

In order to live in resurrection, we must first die. Without death, there can be no resurrection. Verse 4 says, "We have been buried therefore with Him through baptism into death." We have been buried into His death. Jesus was first slain and then buried, but we are first buried, and then we die. In baptism we bury living persons into death. However, this death remains in the baptistry. When we come out of the water, we are resurrected. We all need to see a vision of Christ's death and of His resurrection. When He was crucified, we were crucified with Him (Gal. 2:20a). We were all included in Him when He was crucified on the cross. Whoever believes in Him was crucified on the cross at the same time and in the same death. Moreover, when He was resurrected, all of His millions of believers were resurrected with Him (Eph. 2:6; 1 Pet. 1:3).

When we believed, we believed into Him. The preposition *into* signifies that one person is now in the other. We were in Adam, but when we believed in Christ Jesus, we believed into Him. We have been transferred. Now we are in Christ, who died and resurrected. Because we are in Him, whatever He experienced has become our history. We died in Christ almost two thousand years ago, and we were also buried with Him in His tomb. Now we are in His resurrection. Therefore, we should not live in our old life. That old life was terminated and even buried. Now we should live in the resurrected life, in the resurrection of Christ.

Husbands and wives who have exulting faces are living in the life of Christ. The expression of this life is resurrection. The resurrection of Christ is the expression of something new. Therefore, to live in the life of Christ is to live in the newness of life. Romans 6 shows us that we are dead and buried and are now in His resurrection. When we live in this resurrection, we live in the newness of Christ's life. If we desire to be saved daily and constantly, we must realize that we are persons who are dead and buried. But we are no longer in the tomb; we are now in resurrection.

When the Lord Jesus resurrected from the tomb, He left behind the linen cloths and the handkerchief that bound Him (John 20:5-7). When Peter came to the tomb and saw them lying in a good order, he realized that the Lord had resurrected. All the things left in the tomb were a testimony to the Lord's resurrection. The cloths and the handkerchief signify the old creation, which the Lord wore into the tomb. He was crucified with the old creation and buried with it. When He resurrected, He left the old creation in His tomb, and He became the first-fruit, the germination, of God's new creation. All of the old creation, including us, was terminated and left in the tomb of Christ. We were a part of the old creation, typified by the linen and the handkerchief which the Lord Jesus wore. We were all buried with Him, and when He resurrected, He left us in the tomb. Now we should remain in the tomb. The termination and burial of the old creation is fully signified by baptism. The old creation was buried in the baptistry.

To display an unpleasant face to our spouse is to revive the buried old man. We should not allow the old man to return to live with us. If we allow the old man to return, we are not living in newness of life. Rather, we are in the oldness of death. We must live a life in resurrection, and this life is based upon the all-inclusive death of Christ. The Christian story is a wonderful story. There is the historical side of the story, which consists of the facts, and there is also the experiential side, the side of our daily life. According to history, the old man was buried, but in our daily life, the old man is still lodging with us. A house is a lodging place for living persons, while a tomb is for dead persons. In a sense, our body is a tomb for the old creation. We have to tell the old man, "I am not your house for you to live in. I am your tomb for you to be buried in."

THE WAY TO EXPERIENCE LIFE

Romans 8 gives us the way to experience the life of Christ. In this chapter there are five critical verses related to life. Verse 2 speaks of the Spirit of life. Verse 10 says that if Christ is in us, our human spirit is life. Verse 6 says that the mind set on the spirit is life. Verse 11 says that the indwelling Spirit gives life even to our mortal body. The Spirit is life, our human spirit is life, our mind is life, and even our body is life. Finally, verse 13 says that we need to put to death by the indwelling Spirit the practices of the body. If we do this, our entire being will live. These verses speak on the one hand of the Holy Spirit and on the other hand of our human spirit. These two spirits are mingled together as one spirit. The dispensing of the Triune God into us makes us life in the three parts of our being: first in our spirit, second in our mind, the main part of our soul, and third in our body. We are becoming persons in life. In this way, we are being saved in the life of Christ minute by minute, and we live a life in resurrection. Moreover, the element of resurrection is the newness of this life. Now, after being reconciled to God, we are being saved in such a life, the life that has passed through death and burial and today is in resurrection.

QUESTIONS AND ANSWERS

Question: Romans 6:4 says that we have been buried with Christ through baptism into death. Then verse 5 says that we shall be in the likeness of His resurrection. However, note 3 of Philippians 3:10 in the Recovery Version *says, "With Christ, the sufferings and death came first, followed by the resurrection; with us, the power of His resurrection comes first, then the fellowship of His sufferings and conformity to His death." In what order do we experience death and resurrection?*

Answer: In Romans 6 death is first, followed by resurrection. According to fact, resurrection is based upon death. The facts are our history: first we died with Christ, and then we resurrected. However, Philippians 3 is not according to fact but according to experience. In our experience, resurrection is followed by death. The power of resurrection is Christ Himself. Since we have Him within us, we have the power of resurrection. By this power we are enabled to live a life on the path of Christ's death, in the mold of His death.

Question: Often when situations surprise us, there is a reaction of the old man within us. How should we deal with that reaction? Should we simply say "No" to the old man at that time, or must we remain "on the mountaintop" at all times in order to be prepared for every situation?

Answer: The Lord Jesus with His three disciples did not remain on the mountaintop for very long (Matt. 17:1-8). When they came down from the mountain, they found a case of demon possession (vv. 14-21). We must realize that our environment fluctuates all the time. The Lord Jesus is on the mountaintop, and He is also in the valley. According to His presence, there is no difference between the mountain and the valley. He always remains the same. We should not care for the environment; we should care only for His presence. We do not live according to the environment. For the unbelievers, the only aspect of their experience is the environment. We believers, however, live according to the Lord's presence. This requires a daily experience of the Lord. If we have the adequate experience of the Lord every day, we will remain the same when the environment changes.

THE EXPERIENCE AND GROWTH IN LIFE

MESSAGE SEVENTEEN

THE EXPERIENCE OF LIFE

(9)

Scripture Reading: 2 Cor. 3:15-18

TRANSFORMATION
AND THE GROWTH IN LIFE

In previous messages we have considered Romans 6 and 8 and the entire book of Philippians in regard to the experience and growth in life. In this message we will consider how transformation is related to our growth in life. The measure of our growth in life depends upon the measure of our transformation.

Second Corinthians 3:15 through 18 says, "But unto this day, whenever Moses is read, a veil lies on their heart; but whenever it turns to the Lord, the veil is taken away. And the Lord is the Spirit, and where the Spirit of the Lord is, there is freedom. And we all with unveiled face, beholding and reflecting as a mirror the glory of the Lord, are being transformed into the same image from glory to glory, even as from the Lord Spirit." The main point of these verses is transformation.

BEING TRANSFERRED FOR TRANSFORMATION

In chapters three and four of 2 Corinthians, Paul primarily deals with the ministry of the Old Testament and the ministry of the New Testament. In this portion of chapter three, he deals with the matter of transformation. God has transferred us from the Old Testament ministry to the New Testament ministry. This transfer is for transformation. Because we have been transferred, we can be transformed.

The Turned-away Heart Being
the Veil under the Old Testament

Under the Old Testament ministry, a veil lies over the heart. Second Corinthians 3:14-15 says, "For until the present day the same veil remains at the reading of the old cove-nant....But unto this day, whenever Moses is read, a veil lies on their heart." The "present day" refers to the time of Paul's writing his Epistle to the Corinthians when Paul was carrying out the New Testament ministry. Until that time the Jews still had a veil upon their heart whenever they read the Old Testament writings. Today, two thousand years later, it is still the same among most of the Jews.

Apparently the Jewish rabbis and the Jewish seeking ones love God, but their love of God is according to their traditions. According to a recent news report, the Jewish religious lead-ers charged their people not to set foot on the Temple Mount, where the site for the temple is presumed to be, lest they acci-dentally step on the site of the ancient Holy of Holies and offend God. This is an example of their devotion to God accord-ing to their traditions. They love God completely according to their traditions and without any light from the Lord. They read the Old Testament, but they cannot see any light.

Many of the Jews are very devoted, but they are also thor-oughly veiled. Apparently their heart loves the Lord; actually their heart is still turned away from the Lord. In 2 Corinthi-ans 3:15-16 Paul says, "A veil lies on their heart; but whenever it turns to the Lord, the veil is taken away." "It" in verse 16 refers to the "heart" in verse 15. This means that whenever the heart turns to the Lord, the veil is taken away. The veil is their turned-away heart. Because the direction of their heart is wrong, they are veiled. If our angle in viewing an object is wrong, we cannot see anything. We have to adjust our view, then we will be able to see clearly. Our self with the wrong angle is the veil. When we turn ourselves to the right angle, we see. At Paul's time many of the Jews were seeking God, but the direction of their hearts was wrong. Because they were not in the proper direction, they became a veil to themselves. Therefore, Paul said, "Whenever it [the heart] turns to the Lord, the veil is taken away" (2 Cor. 3:16).

The Triune God Processed to Become the Life-giving Spirit in the New Testament

In the New Testament, the veil is taken away and the Lord is the Spirit (2 Cor. 3:17). In the Old Testament, the Lord as the Spirit was not there because the Triune God had not yet passed through any processes. In the Old Testament, before the processes of incarnation, human living, death, and resurrection, the Triune God remained the "raw" God. But in the New Testament, having passed through all these processes, the Lord became a life-giving Spirit (1 Cor. 15:45b). Now He is no longer "raw"; He is the processed Triune God. In resurrection the Lord as the last Adam became the life-giving Spirit, not only with divinity but also with humanity. His being the last Adam indicates His humanity. The first Adam was only a created man, but the last Adam is God incarnate, the very God with His humanity who became a life-giving Spirit.

THE HISTORY OF THE TRIUNE GOD

Incarnation, Crucifixion, and Resurrection Consummating in the Spirit

God becoming a man and this man becoming the life-giving Spirit are a great mystery. We can never fully understand this mystery. The Triune God passing through the processes of incarnation, human living, death, and resurrection in order to give life to us is the most wonderful story in the whole universe. This story is a real history. The Triune God Himself became a man of flesh. He lived on this earth for thirty-three and a half years. He then voluntarily went to the cross and was crucified for six hours to accomplish an all-inclusive death. He then was buried, and three days later He walked out of death in resurrection. When He lived on this earth, walked to the cross, was crucified, buried, and resurrected, He was in humanity. He carried out all these things in His humanity. By such a process His humanity was uplifted. He was transferred and transformed from flesh into the Spirit.

His being transferred involved transformation, a transformation of humanity into divinity. This was the procedure for His being "sonized." Sonizing is a transformation, a transfer, in which the Lord as a person with divinity and humanity became *the* Spirit. The Lord being the Spirit (2 Cor. 3:17) implies all of this. The greatest history among all the histories is the history of God becoming a man and being transferred and transformed to be *the* Spirit. The Spirit is the consummation of the divine history.

The Enlargement, Expansion, and Increase of Christ

We also share in this divine history which has not yet been completed. The book of Acts is an ongoing history of Jesus through His believers; therefore, it does not have an end or a conclusion because it is still being written today. It is a history of God Himself in Christ with His believers as His expansion, enlargement, and increase.

We believers are a part of the enlarged Christ. This is the revelation Paul received when the Lord spoke to him from the heavens as Paul traveled to Damascus in Acts 9. When Paul persecuted the believers of Jesus, he never thought that he was persecuting Jesus. But when the Lord Jesus spoke to him, He said, "Saul, Saul, why are you persecuting Me?" (v. 4). This word indicates that the followers of Jesus become a part of Jesus Himself.

TRANSFERRED AND TRANSFORMED

In 2 Corinthians 3:16-18 there are five items which show us how to be transferred and how to be transformed. First, the heart turns to the Lord. Second, the veil is taken away. Third, the Lord is the Spirit. Fourth, where the Spirit of the Lord is, there is freedom. Finally, we are transformed by beholding and reflecting the glory of the Lord.

Transferred from the Old Testament Ministry to the New Testament Ministry

To be transferred is to be transferred from the Old Testament ministry to the New Testament ministry. The main

thought in 2 Corinthians 3 is not that we have been transferred out of Adam into Christ. This is the thought of
Romans 6—8. Rather, the thought here is that we have been
transferred from the old writings, the old teaching, which is
according to the letter, to the New Testament teaching which
is according to the Spirit. Thus, we have been transferred
from the old ministry to the new ministry.

Teaching the New Testament according to the Old Testament Ministry versus Teaching the Bible according to the New Testament Ministry

The New Testament is often taught as history according to
the Old Testament ministry in letter without any real light.
This kind of teaching results in death (2 Cor. 3:6). The New
Testament in one person's hand may be one kind of book, but
in another person's hand it may be a completely different
book. The book of Acts in the hands of some in Christianity
has been made to be something of the Old Testament in letter.
As a youth I studied the book of Acts in a Christian school. I
was only taught such things as the distance from Samaria to
Jerusalem and the history of the Samaritans. These things
are certainly in the book of Acts, but such a study of Acts is
only according to the letter. When the book of Acts is taught
according to the New Testament ministry, Christ is ministered into you with light, life, and grace. This ministry of
Christ will result in the kingdom of God, which is the church
today (Rom. 14:17). The goal of my ministry is to help you to
be transferred out of the teachings of the letter into the teachings of the Spirit. The notes in the *Recovery Version* of the
New Testament have been written with this goal.

Today we are in the New Testament age and apparently
under the New Testament ministry. Often, however, we are
not actually under the New Testament ministry. Though we
read the New Testament, most of the time our being may be
in the Old Testament age and under the Old Testament ministry. Therefore, we must realize our need to turn our heart
to the Lord every day. When we turn our heart to the Lord,
the veil is taken away, we see the Lord clearly, and we are

attracted to Him. The more we see of Him, the more we love Him. The Lord we love is the Spirit today, and where the Spirit is, there is freedom.

TRANSFORMED BY BEHOLDING AND REFLECTING THE LORD

In 2 Corinthians 3:18 we behold and reflect as a mirror the glory of the Lord with an unveiled face. The more a mirror beholds an object, the more the mirror reflects the object. The mirror is transformed into the image of its object. We as the mirrors beholding and reflecting the glory of the Lord are being transformed into the image of the Lord.

TRANSFORMATION BEING A METABOLIC PROCESS

Transformation is a metabolic process. First, we are transferred from the Old Testament ministry to the New Testament ministry. Then in this transfer, we are transformed. In the transfer itself, nothing metabolic takes place, but in transformation something metabolic happens. Transformation is a metabolic process whereby a new element is added to the original element. Water as one element can be transformed by the addition of another element such as lemon. Water and lemon can be mingled together. This mingling is a transformation. The mingling of water and lemon does not fully illustrate transformation because no action of life is at work.

As believers we have our human life, and the Lord who is the Spirit gives the divine life to us. These two lives are being mingled together. In this mingling, there is the action of life on the part of both lives. This action of life from both parties eventually becomes the one action of metabolism. When the two living elements are added together, a metabolic process results, issuing in transformation.

In 2 Corinthians 3:18 the King James Version uses the word *changed*. The word *transformed* should be used here rather than *changed* because the Greek word here is *metamorphoo*. The word *change* by itself does not indicate metabolism or transformation. If my face is pale, I can change its appearance by adding some pink makeup to it. This is a change but not a transformation, because nothing metabolic has taken place. But if I eat well by including some vitamins in my diet and sleep well, my pale face will eventually be changed into a face full of pink color. This is transformation.

TRANSFORMED BY THE MINGLING
OF HUMANITY WITH DIVINITY

In our transfer from Adam to Christ, from the Old Testament to the New Testament, from the old teaching to the new teaching, and from the Old Testament ministry to the New Testament ministry, the divine element was added into our being. Now the mingling together of these two elements has produced the metabolic result of transformation. The way the divine element is constantly added into us is by our beholding and reflecting the Lord with an unveiled face. This is why we need to have morning watch each day. Following morning watch, throughout the day we still need to behold and reflect the Lord who is the life-giving Spirit. As the life-giving Spirit, He gives us freedom. As we behold and reflect, we receive the divine element which results in transformation.

TRANSFORMED INTO THE IMAGE
OF THE GLORIFIED CHRIST

We are being transformed into the image of the glorified Christ. Our image, which is the expression of what we are, becomes the same as the glorified Christ. He is holy and we are also holy. He is loving and we are loving. He is patient and we are also patient. He is full of dignity and so are we. This is the growth in life by transformation.

Transformation is from the Lord Spirit (2 Cor. 3:18). The compound title *Lord Spirit* refers to one person. Today, our Triune God is the Lord Spirit. It is from Him that transformation, the mingling of divinity with our humanity, issues forth.

In summary, transformation is to receive the divine element into our being by beholding and reflecting the Lord, which causes a metabolic process to occur. This metabolic process is transformation, the mingling of humanity with divinity, to express the same image of the glorious Christ who is the God-man.

THE EXPERIENCE AND GROWTH IN LIFE

MESSAGE EIGHTEEN

THE GROWTH IN LIFE

(9)

Scripture Reading: 2 Cor. 4:6-12, 16

THE MINISTRY AND MINISTERS OF THE NEW COVENANT

Second Corinthians may be considered as the autobiography of Paul. In the first several chapters of this book there are many deep points concerning the life and work of Paul and his co-workers as ministers of the New Testament. They were not merely taught, edified, or instructed in the New Testament ministry. They were constituted with it. In the apostle's speaking concerning their ministry for God's new covenant, five very significant and expressive metaphors are used to illustrate how they, as ministers of the new covenant, and their ministry are constituted, how they behave and live, and how their ministry is carried out.

Captives of Christ

First, the ministers of the new covenant were captives in a triumphant procession for the celebration of Christ's victory (2:14a). They were defeated and they were captured. From the day that Paul, as Saul of Tarsus, was defeated and captured by Christ, he was a captive under Christ's power and authority. On the one hand, we have been freed by Christ; we are released people, who now have our freedom and liberty. On the other hand, however, we have been captured by Christ. Every person freed by Christ is a captive of Christ. If something of Christ is to be transfused into us, we must be captives. Today in America, everyone treasures their liberty, freedom, and human rights, and no one wants to be considered a captive. We, however, are the captives of Christ.

Incense-bearers
to Scatter the Fragrance of Christ

As captives, the ministers of the new covenant are also the incense-bearers to scatter the fragrance of Christ as the conquering general (2:14b-16). We are not only Christ's captives, but also His incense-bearers, scattering His fragrance to others.

Letters Written with Christ

As apostles, Paul and his co-workers were letters, epistles written with Christ as the content (3:1-3). The Spirit of God was the "ink," the element with which Paul was written upon to be a letter of Christ. He was a living letter written by the Holy Spirit with all the realities of Christ as the writing element. Today, when we read Paul's autobiography, we can see Christ. We can read Christ in him. What is written in Paul's Epistles is nothing but Christ. Christ is conveyed to the readers in every book he wrote.

Certain Christians emphasize that we should not exalt any man. However, for nineteen centuries Paul has been appreciated very much. Paul is always associated with Christ because Paul is Christ's letter. When we read him, we see Christ. It is difficult not to refer to Paul when we speak about Christ. The fourteen Epistles of Paul constitute half of the twenty-seven books of the New Testament. Without these fourteen Epistles, the New Testament would not be complete (Col. 1:25).

When the Corinthians were sinners, not knowing Christ, Paul came to them and brought them to Christ. He begot them in Christ through the gospel and became their spiritual father (1 Cor. 4:15). In a sense, Paul begot us also. In the past sixty years, the most help I have received from the New Testament has been from Paul's Epistles. Without these fourteen Epistles, there would be a great lack. Because Christ is all-inclusive and mysterious, the four Gospels are not adequate to make Him clear to us. It would be difficult for us to know who Christ is without Paul's Epistles.

In the fourteen Epistles, we see Christ to a much greater extent than what is portrayed in the four Gospels. We see the all-inclusive, mysterious Christ, who is the mystery of God (Col. 2:2) and who produces the mystery of Christ, the church (Eph. 3:4). The most striking point of Paul's Epistles is that in them he opens up the eternal and universal mystery. God has a mystery which He planned in eternity past, but the four Gospels do not speak much concerning God's eternal plan as the mystery of the entire universe. Paul, however, unveils to us the mystery of the all-inclusive Christ as the Head for the producing of the Body. The church as the Body of Christ is presented only by Paul, not by Peter, John, or any of the other writers of the New Testament. We are indebted to the writings of Paul.

Paul was constituted with Christ and was a living letter of Christ. Since Paul's writings express what he was, they are also a letter of Christ. Whenever we read Paul's Epistles, we read Christ. Paul's Epistles do not convey mainly himself, but the very Christ with whom he was constituted to such an extent that he could say, "It is no longer I who live, but Christ lives in me" (Gal. 2:20). Paul lived and did many things, yet it was no longer he but Christ. When we read Paul's Epistles, we are reading him, yet what we see is not Paul himself but Christ as his constituent. We also should be constituted with Christ. In a sense, the name of Christ should be a part of our name, because when people read us, they see Christ. It is no more we, but Christ who lives in us. To us, to live is not ourselves but Christ (Phil. 1:21). Christ is our person and the reality of our person. In this sense, we are not Americans or Chinese; we are Christ.

Mirrors Beholding and Reflecting
the Glory of Christ

Paul and his co-workers were also mirrors beholding and reflecting with an unveiled face the glory of Christ in order to be transformed into His glorious image (2 Cor. 3:18). Man was made in the image of God (Gen. 1:26), and Colossians 1:15

says that Christ is the image of the invisible God. The glorious image unveiled in 2 Corinthians 3 is the divine image in Genesis 1:26. However, at the time of Genesis 1:26, Christ did not have the elements of incarnation, humanity, His all-inclusive, wonderful death, and the wonderful resurrection. These elements have now been added to Christ by the process through which the Triune God has passed. Now the image of God is not only the image of divinity, but the image of divinity mingled with humanity and constituted with the all-inclusive death and the wonderful resurrection.

Earthen Vessels
Containing the Excellent Treasure

The apostles were also earthen vessels to contain the Christ of glory as the excellent treasure (2 Cor. 4:7). Verse 7 says, "But we have this treasure in earthen vessels, that the excellence of the power may be of God and not of us." The earthen vessels are worthless and fragile, but a priceless treasure is contained in the worthless vessels. This treasure enters into the vessels by God's shining. When God shines, the treasure is infused into the earthen vessels. The content of this treasure is divinity mingled with humanity, constituted with His wonderful, all-inclusive death and resurrection. We need to enjoy the constituents of this treasure. We should enjoy divinity, humanity, and even death. There are two kinds of death in the universe. One is the death of Adam, and the other is the death of Christ. We hate the death of Adam, but we love the wonderful, marvelous, all-inclusive death of Christ.

The excellent power of the treasure is manifested in the earthen vessels. Verse 8 says, "We are afflicted in every way, but not straitened; perplexed, but not despairing." Being afflicted in every way indicates affliction in every kind of suffering, but it is not merely suffering. Being afflicted in every way indicates the all-inclusive death of Christ, but not being straitened is resurrection. Likewise, being perplexed indicates death, but not despairing is resurrection. Verse 9 says, "Persecuted, but not forsaken; cast down, but not destroyed." Being persecuted and cast down again indicate death, but not being forsaken and not being destroyed refer to resurrection.

Verses 10-12 say, "Always bearing about in the body the putting to death of Jesus, that the life also of Jesus might be manifested in our body. For we who live are always being delivered unto death for Jesus' sake, that the life also of Jesus might be manifested in our mortal flesh. So then death operates in us, but life in you." The death for Jesus' sake is the glorious, wonderful, loveable death of Christ. The life of Jesus is resurrection.

Earthen vessels containing a treasure is the last metaphor used to describe the ministers of the new covenant and their ministry. This portion of the Word leads us into the real experience of Christ's death and resurrection. We are the earthen vessels, yet we have a treasure in us. This demonstrates the excellence of the power of the treasure in death and resurrection. Christ's power is not only manifested in resurrection but also in death. The four Gospels show us how Christ passed through a long journey of death, but He was not put down by death; the many aspects of death could not restrain Him. He had the power to overcome death. In death the power of Christ was greatly manifested. In His resurrection His power was also manifested. There was no way to subdue Paul because as an earthen vessel he had Christ as the treasure within him. In this way, the excellent power of the treasure was manifested. This was not of man but of God.

Verse 16 says, "Wherefore we do not lose heart, but if indeed our outward man is decaying, yet our inward man is being renewed day by day." Decay indicates death, but renewal is resurrection. Our afflictions may cause us to lose heart, but we have to thank and worship the Lord for our afflictions. The Lord allows us to pass through afflictions so that our inward man may be renewed day by day.

We are all the captives of Christ. Therefore, we are Christ's incense-bearers, scattering, dispensing, the fragrance of Christ to others. We are also letters of Christ written by the Spirit, not to display ourselves, but to display ourselves with Christ. In this sense, "Christ" should be a part of our name. We are also mirrors, and we are vessels to contain Christ as the treasure, that day after day we may express the all-inclusive death of Christ and the resurrection power. How much of this treasure we have in us is indicated by how much we express Christ in His all-inclusive death and resurrection.

QUESTIONS AND ANSWERS

Question: Being afflicted, perplexed, persecuted, and cast down and the decaying of our outward man are all aspects of the death in Adam. However, 2 Corinthians 4:10 speaks of "always bearing about in the body the putting to death of Jesus." Are there two different kinds of death, or are these the same death?

Answer: The death that takes place in Adam is ugly, but the same death, when it takes place in Christ, is lovely. Adam died, and Christ also died. However, with one the death was ugly, but with the other the death was lovely. With unbelievers, no affliction is good, but with us, the believers, all afflictions are very good. If persecution befalls us, it is wonderful, but if it befalls an unbelieving relative, it is terrible. All the negative items in verses 8 through 12 are different aspects of the death of Christ. We may call them sufferings, but according to Philippians 3:10, sufferings are a part of Christ's death. Philippians 3:10 says, "To know Him and the power of His resurrection and the fellowship of His sufferings, being conformed to His death." The fellowship, the participation, of His sufferings is the participation in His death. To participate in His death is to be conformed to His death. Every day we are afflicted, perplexed, cast down, and persecuted, and our outward man is decaying, being consumed. These are different aspects of Christ's death. When we are suffering these things, Christ's death is being applied to us. Through this death the life of Christ is manifested.

THE EXPERIENCE AND GROWTH IN LIFE

MESSAGE NINETEEN

THE EXPERIENCE OF LIFE

(10)

Scripture Reading: Phil. 2:12-14; 3:10

In the past several weeks, we have seen the experience and growth in life in the books of Romans, Philippians, and 2 Corinthians. My burden in giving these messages is that you would gain the crucial factors and elements concerning the experience and growth in life, not just some general knowledge.

OUR NEED TO EXPERIENCE THE CRUCIAL FACTORS OF CHRIST, HIS DEATH, AND HIS RESURRECTION

Some of the crucial factors and elements for our experience and growth in life are mentioned in Philippians 2:12-14. We must work out our salvation by dealing with murmurings and reasonings. In verses 12 through 14, murmurings and reasonings are mentioned with the two great factors of God's operation and our working out of God's salvation. It seems that murmurings and reasonings are rather small and insignificant, but in our experience of life, these are two very important items with which we need to deal.

Everyone murmurs and reasons. To deal with murmurings and reasonings is not very easy, because only a dead person does not murmur. To make a decision not to murmur does not work. Although it is difficult to refrain from murmurings and reasonings, we must realize that as long as we murmur and reason, we are defeated in working out our salvation in our daily life. In order to work out this salvation, we must pray, "Lord, grant me to know You and the power of Your resurrection and the fellowship of Your sufferings, being conformed to Your death." While the Lord Jesus lived on this earth, He never murmured, because He lived a crucified life, a life which was always under the cross. The way to be delivered from murmurings and reasonings is just to die, but we cannot crucify ourselves. Brother Nee once said that no one can commit suicide by crucifixion because crucifixion requires another person to be involved. We need to know the fellowship of His sufferings, that is, to participate in the sufferings of Christ.

In married life, if one is not careful concerning murmurings and reasonings, the issue may be separation and divorce. In a sense, married life represents all kinds of corporate life. When a number of people work together, speak together, or play together, they are considered a team. A married couple or a family may also be considered a team. The church life is a team life.

The Apostle Paul aspired to know three crucial factors: Christ, the power of His resurrection, and conformity to the death of Christ (Phil. 3:10). Without these three factors, we do not have the reality of life. Some philosophers, such as Confucius, taught a great deal about having a high standard of ethics. But without Christ, His resurrection power, and His death, all of these teachings are merely vain talk. Paul's teaching was not in vain, because his teaching was full of these three factors. These three factors—Christ, His resurrection power, and His death—must not remain only historical to us; they must become our experience and daily salvation.

QUESTIONS AND ANSWERS

Question: Sometimes as I enjoy the Lord, I receive His grace, and when situations arise, I am able to overcome them to remain in fellowship with the Lord. But at other times, when the Lord seems to be very distant, a situation comes in, I react, and it seems to take some length of time to restore my once peaceful situation. Is this normal?

Answer: The Christian life is not a philosophical life of reasonings. The Christian life is a life of the three factors I have mentioned earlier. It is a living Person with His history of death and resurrection. This Person with His history should be our experience today. We should forget about all kinds of philosophy. Today most Christian teachers have turned biblical teachings into something philosophical. Though I would agree that the Bible is the most philosophical book, the most thoughtful book, to make its teaching a philosophy is a big mistake. The Bible does not reveal different kinds of philosophies. It unveils a living Person, who is *the* Spirit today as the very consummation of the processed Triune God. This One is our need.

There is a great deal of scientific knowledge concerning electricity. The need in our daily life is not this knowledge, but the power of electricity. In the same way, Christ with His death and resurrection should not be a philosophy to us, but something living and experiential. In Philippians 3 Paul sought to know Christ as a living Person, to participate in His sufferings, and to be conformed to His death. This was not a philosophy to Paul, but a living Person with two living points. We must have the same desire, even the same vision, as Paul. When we see such a vision, many of our improper prayers and foolish seeking will come to an end. Our need is to be unveiled to see a vision of Christ and His death and resurrection.

I am concerned that many of the young people will merely learn things in this training as they would in a school with a "textbook," without really seeing something. My real burden is to help you see something. As you read this message, I hope that you could see the living Person of Christ, His death, and His resurrection again and again.

A hymn such as #642 in *Hymns* does not merely teach us. On the contrary, it unveils spiritual reality to us. Our need is not just to learn doctrines, but to open ourselves to the Lord so that we can see something. We should pray, "Lord, I open myself to You. I want to see more of You as an all-inclusive Person. Show me how Your all-inclusive death and resurrection includes me." Then as we listen to the speaking concerning Christ, we will begin to see something. What we see becomes a reality within us. Then we live by what we have seen.

The death and resurrection of Christ must become a vision to us. On the cross, not only was Christ crucified there, but also all the existing things in the universe were crucified with Him. He was on the cross representing the entire old creation, so when He died, we died with Him. His death was our death. Likewise, when He resurrected, we also resurrected with Him to be the people of His new creation. His resurrection was the birth, the germination, of the new creation. Christ is an all-inclusive Person, so His resurrection, based upon His all-inclusive death, is also all-inclusive. My burden is to help you see this vision.

Vision comes from hearing and hearing comes from speaking. In Christianity, the subtle enemy has cut off the proper speaking of Christ and His death and resurrection. But praise the Lord that He is still speaking today. As long as He speaks and you hear, you also see a vision. Once you see something, you also enjoy the reality. The reality is mainly composed of three factors: the all-inclusive Christ as a living Person, His all-inclusive death, and His all-inclusive resurrection. When we see these factors, we are brought into the realization and experience of them.

Question: Having seen something of Christ and His all-inclusive death and resurrection, why does it seem so difficult to experience these things?

Answer: The reason for this is that our vision is often very vague. We see something, but not so clearly. We must realize that genuine believing is based upon what we see. When we preach the gospel, we must hold the realization that we are presenting something of reality to people. Our speaking is the presentation of reality. When our listeners hear our presentation, they see something and believe. What they see becomes their faith, their believing. The problem is that often our speaking is weak and the hearing is also weak; therefore, the believing and seeing become very weak. The strength of what we see and believe depends upon the strength of our hearing. Whether our hearing is strong or not depends upon the strength of the speaking.

Question: Does the vision of Christ and His death and resurrection come suddenly as a one-time experience or does it come gradually over some period of time?

Answer: Often it is difficult to determine whether what we see today is a sudden revelation or something which has come gradually through our experience. As we are walking down a certain street, we are able to see the things on that street because we are in the position to see them. One day we see one thing, and another day we see something more. In the same principle, as we attend the meetings of the church, we may not see very much at first. But as we continue to attend the meetings and hear the speaking, gradually we begin to see something month after month and year after year.

We do not often have the experience of seeing something in a sudden way. Actually, according to my experience, the sudden or instant vision is not very valuable. The most valuable vision is something which has been built up within you. If from the day you are saved, you build up a habit of always being in the meetings, big or small, year-round, this will constitute something of a vision within you, which will become something very stable within you. Through the meetings something is sown into you. The accumulation of what has been sown into you is your seeing, your vision. To gain such a vision requires time. We should not expect to see the vision of Christ, His death, and His resurrection in a sudden way. Gradually, as we go on in our experience with the Lord, we see more.

The disciples, especially Peter, are a good illustration of this. Many teachers and students of the Bible throughout church history have tried to determine when Peter was saved. On several occasions Peter had some very significant experiences with the Lord. The first experience was when he was brought to the Lord by his brother, Andrew (John 1:40-42). On this occasion, the Lord changed his name from Simon to Peter, a stone. This experience, however, did not change Peter very much, because shortly thereafter he went back to fishing. Then the Lord went to the sea of Galilee and called Peter as he was casting a net into the sea (Matt. 4:18-19). The Lord attracted him, perhaps by the miracle recorded in Luke 5:4-11. At one moment he was casting a net for fish, and the next moment, having been called by the Lord Jesus, he began to follow the Lord. After perhaps three years of following the Lord, Peter and the other disciples were led by the Lord to Caesarea Philippi (Matt. 16:13). The Lord asked them, "Who do you say that I am?" (v. 15). Peter responded, "You are the Christ, the Son of the living God" (v. 16). This was another significant experience. After these experiences, Peter denied the Lord three times, even before the Lord's face (Luke 22:54-61). And on the day of Christ's resurrection, the angel specifically mentioned that Peter should be told about the Lord's resurrection (Mark 16:7). Then on the evening of the day of resurrection, the Lord came back to breathe Himself into the disciples (John 20:22).

Through these experiences it is difficult to determine when Peter was regenerated. It seems that Peter might have been regenerated when he made the declaration in Matthew 16:16 that Jesus is the Son of the living God. However, Peter was undoubtedly regenerated after the Lord breathed Himself into the disciples. The earlier experiences seem to have been an accumulation consummating in the experience in John 20:22.

In principle, it is the same with us today. Because our experiences of the Lord accumulate over time, we may have the feeling that our experiences some years ago were not as genuine as they are today. Though our experiences seem to be very sudden, they are actually an accumulation over many years. The things we see today which seem to be rather sudden will be recognized, after a few years, as having only been steps in a process of accumulation.

Often it may seem that we have not seen or experienced very much, when we have actually seen and experienced a great deal without realizing it. On the other hand, we often think that we have seen something, when in reality we have seen and experienced very little. As a result, we are easily deceived. The best way is simply to walk on the pathway of life, day by day, without analyzing very much. Again, the disciples are good examples of this. Peter and the other disciples followed the Lord somewhat foolishly and ignorantly for three and a half years. It is doubtful that Peter was very clear concerning anything he saw during those years with the Lord. He seemed to be clear when he spoke concerning Christ being the Son of the living God, but later when asked whether the Lord paid the temple tax, he answered in a very inaccurate way (Matt. 17:24-27). This exposed that he had not seen very clearly that Jesus as the Son of God is not required to pay such a tax.

As the Lord was going to Jerusalem to be crucified, the disciples also argued among themselves as to which one of them would be the greatest (Mark 9:33-34). They did not care for the Lord or for what He had told them concerning His death and resurrection. It seems that after three and a half years the disciples saw very little and that the time the Lord spent with them was wasted. It even seemed that the sisters, such as Mary Magdalene, Mary the mother of Jesus, and the mother of James and John, saw much more than the brothers. Although this may be true, actually, all but Judas received something from the Lord in those years.

We must realize that any time we spend with the Lord is never a waste. The more time we spend with the Lord, the more we learn, and the more a treasure is accumulated within our being. Therefore, we must continue to pursue the Lord according to a good routine. Such a routine includes morning watch every morning, walking by the Spirit each day, and attending the meetings regularly. In spite of all our failures, we should still keep such a routine. This kind of exercise before the Lord will never be a waste.

Question: I have a question concerning ministering to others. Many times when I am in the home meetings and the atmosphere is living, I share something with the new believers which is right in doctrine but the flavor seems to be me. Will there be a time in our ministry to others when we sense that the Lord has a clear way through us without any flavor of ourselves?

Answer: Our feelings are just like the weather—extremely variable and untrustworthy. Concerning our ministry, we should just go and minister, not analyzing too much. We should just labor in the home meetings, small group meetings, and big meetings. Eventually, we will see the Lord's blessing and we will reach the goal. According to my experience, quite often I thought that I accomplished very little when I ministered in a certain place. To my feeling, it was a failure. Then a number of years later, quite a number of saints from that place shared with me that they were really helped by the message I had given earlier. On the other hand, when I have shared at other times, I had the feeling that I had reached the third heaven. Eventually, there was not the great result that I expected.

Though many Christians seek so-called spirituality, we must realize that we will eventually be very human. We also must realize that our flavor will be with us even when we enter into the New Jerusalem. The New Testament was written by many writers. Whenever we read Peter's writing, we know that it is Peter, because it has the flavor of Peter. Likewise, when we read Paul's writing, there is the flavor of Paul. Even in the New Jerusalem, we will not lose our personal identity and flavor.

THE EXPERIENCE AND GROWTH IN LIFE

MESSAGE TWENTY

THE GROWTH IN LIFE

(10)

THE ESSENCE OF THE NEW TESTAMENT

What we have covered in this series of messages entitled *The Experience and Growth in Life* is the extract of the entire New Testament. Within every substance there is an essence, the essential constituent of the substance. An apple is substantial, but within this substance there is the apple juice as its essence. It is easy for many readers of the Bible to understand the story of Jesus. However, it is not as easy to see the extract of what the New Testament speaks concerning Jesus. The history of Jesus is the substance of the New Testament, but we need to see the essence of this substance. Some people have obtained doctoral degrees in the study of the Bible, but they may have seen only the substance. They can tell you what is taught in the four Gospels, in the Acts, in the Epistles of Paul, James, Peter, John, and Jude, and in Revelation. They have seen the substance of the New Testament, but very few Bible readers have seen the essence within the New Testament. If we see the essence of the New Testament, we will rejoice. The essence of the New Testament is the mingling of the divine Spirit with our human spirit. These two spirits are mingled as one (1 Cor. 6:17).

The Divine Spirit

The divine Spirit is the consummation of the processed Triune God dispensing Himself into our being. The elements of this Spirit are the Triune God—the Father, the Son, and the Spirit—with the human nature which was added to Him in incarnation, the human living of thirty-three and a half

years, the all-inclusive death which He accomplished in crucifixion, and the all-powerful resurrection. Such a realization
of the Spirit is the divine revelation of the sixty-six books of
the Bible. At the conclusion of the entire Bible, Revelation
22:17 says, "The Spirit and the bride say, Come!" If we have
not seen the essence of the Bible, it is difficult to understand
this verse. Most readers of the New Testament realize that
the Spirit in this verse is the Holy Spirit. However, to merely
see this is to see the substance and not the essence of the
Spirit. If we have seen the essence of the Spirit, we will realize that the Spirit is not simple. We need the entire Bible of
sixty-six books to expound the truth of the Spirit.

The Spirit is the consummation of the processed Triune
God. The term consummation implies certain procedures,
or processes. The processes through which the Triune God
has passed may be compared to cooking. Before His incarnation, the Triune God was the "raw" God. He was the divine,
eternal Person, without humanity and without human living.
Just as certain spices are added to food in the process of
cooking, many elements such as humanity, becoming flesh
with the human living, were added to the Triune God in these
processes. By passing through these processes, God was
"cooked." Today the God we love and whom we have received
is not the "raw" God, but the "cooked" God. The cooked God
today is Jesus Christ, and Jesus Christ is the consummated
Spirit to be life and everything to His believers (1 Cor. 15:45b).

Our Human Spirit

As we have seen, the extract of the New Testament is the
mingling of the divine Spirit with our human spirit. Our human
spirit is not simple. Our spirit was created with the breath of
God. Genesis 2:7 says, "And the Lord God formed man of the
dust of the ground, and breathed into his nostrils the breath of
life; and man became a living soul." The breath of life in Genesis 2:7 became our human spirit. Proverbs 20:27 says, "The
spirit of man is the lamp of the Lord, searching all his inner-
most parts" (ASV). The Hebrew word for breath in Genesis 2:7
(neshamah) is the same as the word for spirit in Proverbs 20:27.
In the Old Testament, the Hebrew word used most of the time

for the Spirit is *ruach*. The Hebrew word *ruach* and the Greek word *pneuma,* as in John 3:8, mean Spirit, breath, wind, and air. The breath of life in Genesis 2:7 is not the Spirit of God, but something very close to the Spirit of God. Our human spirit originated in the breath of God, so it is very close to God. It is something in our makeup which is nearly the same as God Himself. God is Spirit (John 4:24). Man's spirit is not the Spirit of God, but it is God's breath of life.

The most active, aggressive, and living part of man is his spirit. Without his spirit, man is merely clay without life. Even after man was formed from the dust of the ground, he was still inanimate until God breathed the breath of life into him. Then man became a living soul. Man's life came from God's breathing into him the breath of life. The living soul of man is the product of the breath of life entering into the inanimate man, the clay vessel.

The Two Spirits Mingled Together
as One Spirit

However, through man's fall his spirit was contaminated and defiled and became deadened (Eph. 2:1, 5). When we were dead in our spirit, Jesus, as the embodiment of the very Triune God who became the life-giving Spirit, came to us. We received Him, and He entered into our spirit. The extract of the Triune God, the Spirit, was added to our spirit. This extract is the Triune God, who became a man, lived a human life, died on the cross, and rose from the dead. Many elements are included in this extract, including divinity, humanity, human living, the all-inclusive death, and the all-powerful resurrection. When we received this extract, we received all the elements in it. This extract is in our spirit, causing our deadened spirit to become regenerated. Now in our spirit are the divinity, the uplifted, high standard humanity, the proper human living, the all-inclusive crucifixion, and the all-powerful resurrection. Whether or not we understand the elements of this extract, the extract is still in us, nourishing and energizing us.

In our regenerated spirit is the all-inclusive death of Christ. Our temper, our flesh, our old man, our natural man, and all that we are were all-inclusively dealt with in the all-inclusive death of Christ. Now we need to learn how to apply this death by turning to our spirit and remaining there. Remaining in our spirit is also the way to apply the divinity of the Triune God, the uplifted humanity of Jesus with the highest standard, and the powerful resurrection of Christ. By turning to our spirit and remaining there, we enjoy what we have received and now possess. The cross of Christ today is not on Calvary, but in our spirit. If a brother's wife gives him an unpleasant look, he does not need to consider how to apply the cross of Christ. He only needs to turn to his spirit and remain there. There he will have the enjoyment of the processed Triune God with His divinity, His humanity, His uplifted human living, His all-inclusive death, and His all-powerful resurrection.

The essence of the New Testament is the two spirits, the divine Spirit and the human spirit, mingled together as one spirit. If we see this, we will be different persons, rejoicing continually. It is a wonderful thing that people on the earth can live in and by such a mingled spirit.

Now, let us all sing the short song:

> Turn to your spirit and there remain,
> Enjoy the extract—never the same.
> Turn to your spirit and there remain,
> Enjoy the extract—never the same.

(Tune: *Hymns,* #308, chorus)

THE EXPERIENCE AND GROWTH IN LIFE

MESSAGE TWENTY-ONE

THE EXPERIENCE OF LIFE

(11)

Scripture Reading: Matt. 16:26; Luke 9:25

DISPOSITION AND CHARACTER

In this message we will fellowship about dealing with our disposition and character. The words *disposition* and *character* both have many different denotations in dictionaries and lexicons. We have used these words very much in their spiritual denotations for the last forty to fifty years. In one of the early trainings in Taiwan, we presented thirty points of character which were later published in the book *Character*. Later, we began to stress the matter of our disposition very much. I have discovered that character is the expression of something inward, that is, the matter of disposition. Outwardly it is character, but inwardly it is disposition. To deal with the character but neglect the disposition is futile.

I have used the words *disposition* and *character* in my ministry concerning the spiritual life because I was forced to find terms which would help the saints to understand the soul-life, the self, the "I," and the old man. The terms *natural life* and *natural* have also been used related to the spiritual experiences of dealing with our self. The self is our soulish life, and the soulish life is something natural. In addition to these terms, Paul mentions the old man in Romans 6:6. Each of these terms denotes a certain spiritual reality. With human beings there is something called the self, the soul-life. The soul-life is also called the old man. The self, the soul-life, and the old man are all something natural, something of the natural life.

In our fellowship concerning disposition and character, we

do not use the definitions and denotations which are commonly used in the many dictionaries and lexicons. Rather, we define these terms according to their spiritual significance. Disposition refers to something within our being, and character refers to something in our outward being. Within we have our disposition, and without we have our character. Disposition is what we are within, and character is what we express without. The inward disposition and the outward character are the extract, the essence, of our being. If our character and disposition were taken away, there would be nothing left to our being.

The terms *character* and *disposition* cannot be found in the New Testament, but the facts are implied in verses such as Matthew 16:26 and Luke 9:25. Matthew 16:26 and Luke 9:25 are parallel portions which use self and soul-life as synonyms. Matthew 16:26 says, "For what shall a man be profited if he should gain the whole world, but forfeit his soul-life?" Luke 9:25 says, "For what is a man profited, having gained the whole world, but having lost or forfeited himself?" The soul-life in Matthew 16:26 is the self in Luke 9:25. The soul is the life of the self, and the matters of disposition and character are very much related to both the self and the soul.

Disposition

To illustrate the differences in disposition, we may use different animals, such as a turtle and a rabbit. A turtle walks slowly, and a rabbit runs quickly. Each activity is related to a particular thing within the nature of each animal. This inward thing is what we may call its disposition. The turtle and the rabbit each has its own disposition, its own makeup.

In our Christian experience, there is something within us called our disposition. This disposition is what we are in our makeup. Each of us has a particular and unique disposition. Inwardly in our disposition, we are quite different from one another.

Your disposition denotes what you are in your makeup by birth. Whatever you are by birth is your disposition. If you are slow, you were made slow by birth; being slow is your disposition. Likewise, if you are quick, quickness is your disposition.

One may be silent or talkative; both are matters of inward disposition. Although our disposition is something made by God, yet it still needs to be dealt with by God. This seems to be contradictory—something given by God must be dealt with by God. However, this is very much according to the divine revelation, and it is also confirmed by our experience.

Character

Character refers to our outward expression. The Chinese equivalent to the English word *character* means an outward form which expresses the inner nature. Thus, character is the outward form which expresses our inner being. The disposition is always explicitly expressed in our character. Character is at least a part of the expression of disposition. If you were born slow, slowness is always a part of your outward expression, your character. If you were born humble or proud, humility or pride will be a part of the outward expression, the character, of your person.

Character is composed of about thirty percent nature and of about seventy percent habits. For example, if a child is placed in a Chinese home, he will be cast into a Chinese mold. The same child placed in a family of another nationality will resemble a person of that nationality when he grows up. Our outward character is composed of our nature by birth and our habits by living. To deal with our disposition is to deal with what we are inwardly, but to deal with our character is to deal with what we express outwardly, including what we are inwardly. The intrinsic element of our outward character is our inner nature by birth.

We cannot change our inward nature, but we can change or correct our outward character. A dog cannot be trained to be a cat, but it can be trained to behave like a cat. Many brothers have been trained in the military service. When they first entered the military service, they were not very punctual, but after some training and severe discipline, they were adjusted to be punctual. The military service also trained them not to be so talkative and not to be loose in their expression. This kind of training changed their outward character.

DEALING WITH OUR DISPOSITION AND CHARACTER

Our dealings with sins, sin, the world, and the conscience are superficial dealings, but our dealing with the disposition is the deepest dealing. To deal with sins and sin is relatively easy, but to deal with our disposition and character is very difficult. According to my study of the New Testament, we are charged to make confession of our sins and mistakes (1 John 1:8-9), but there is no charge to confess concerning our disposition or character. Many times our disposition may not be right, but it is difficult to say that it is always sinful. Sometimes we are simply in our disposition and not in anything sinful. However, we must realize that our fallen disposition is close to the edge of the deep well of sin and mistakes. Thus, it is very easy for us to fall into this well.

Dealing with our disposition and character will safeguard us from making mistakes and committing sins. Our mistakes and wrongdoings are closely related to our disposition and character. Because we have a particular kind of disposition, we make mistakes. Similarly, we are prone to make mistakes because we have a certain kind of character.

QUESTIONS AND ANSWERS

Question: Is any part of our disposition related to habit?

Answer: Our character is composed thirty percent of our disposition and seventy percent of our habits. Our character is more troublesome than our disposition because our character is composed of our disposition plus our habits. To deal only with our habits is not sufficient because our habits are only the outward expression of our character. In the Gospels, from the time the Lord first called Peter, the Lord took every opportunity to deal with Peter's character and disposition.

Question: When I use the term "deal with," I mean that something is exposed, eliminated, changed, or replaced. Is this what is meant by dealing with our disposition and character?

Answer: To deal with something has a number of meanings in English usage. It can mean to take care of, to punish, to correct, as well as to get rid of. Since our disposition and character cause problems in our Christian life, we have to deal with, take care of, or correct them, and even put them to death. Here the term *deal with* has both a positive and a negative side.

Question: *What is a practical example of dealing with our disposition?*

Answer: In the New Testament, disposition and character are implied in such terms as *self, soul-life, the old man,* and the *I* in Galatians 2:20. These things are all related to the natural life. However, these terms are too general, and their particular meaning and denotation have been lost. But to say that we must deal with our disposition and character is very particular. Actually, to deal with our disposition means to deal with our self, our old man, our soul-life, and the I.

Question: *Is transformation the addition of God's element to our God-given disposition?*

Answer: In describing our relationship with the Lord, many different kinds of terminology have been used. The terminology may be different, but the fact is the same. However, some terminology is not very accurate and can be very misleading. Some have said that we as Christians live an exchanged life. This terminology is absolutely wrong. It is better to say that we live a grafted life. To live an exchanged life can be illustrated by exchanging a watch for a set of eyeglasses. The watch and the eyeglasses are two different things. But to live a grafted life means that two lives have been grafted, even mingled, together. They have been grafted, but both lives continue to exist. On one hand, we are finished, but on the other hand, we still live, as what is unveiled in Galatians 2:20. We are finished in the death of Christ, and we live in the resurrection of Christ. Thus, even in eternity we will continue to live with the divine element added to, grafted to, and mingled with our being. This does not change our nature or characteristic. Our nature and characteristic will remain forever, with something new and living added.

Before we received Christ, we were just ourselves with our nature and characteristic. After we received Christ, we were still ourselves but with something living and new added. This new and living element did not eliminate our nature. Our being still remains. In eternity we will see and recognize all the brothers and sisters, but they will be much newer and much more living. In the past, before we received Christ, we lived by ourselves; but now we live by Christ who lives in us (Gal. 2:20), not in an old way but in an entirely new way.

Transformation deals mainly with our disposition, and renewal deals mainly with our character. Both transformation and renewal simply mean to deal with our disposition and character. A transformed person will not remain in his old disposition, and a renewed person will not remain in his old character or expression.

Question: Is dealing with our disposition and character different from being changed by the divine dispensing?

Answer: The divine dispensing always works to transform us, not only to correct or change us. To change is just to change yourself by your own effort. To transform indicates something divine, something of the Lord, which you do not have by your habits or birth. By the divine dispensing, a divine element is dispensed into you. This element works in you to transform you. If your countenance is pale, through eating, the element of the food will transform your pale color into a healthy color. This healthy color is a transformed color. Without the divine element dispensed into you, you could only have a change but not transformation.

In order for us to experience this transformation, there is the need of the breaking of our disposition and character because our disposition and character are the greatest obstacles to God's dispensing of Himself into us and to His transforming and renewing work on us.

THE EXPERIENCE AND GROWTH IN LIFE

MESSAGE TWENTY-TWO

THE GROWTH IN LIFE

(11)

Scripture Reading: Matt. 16:21-26

For many years I have observed two great frustrating factors in the Lord's work: ambition and opinion. In human society, ambition is a great problem. Everyone, whether in political, commercial, or educational circles, is seeking after promotion. Even among students in school, there is much competition to be the first in their class. The desire for promotion is ambition. Ambition even creeps into the Lord's work. In the church life, there may be an ambition in some brothers for the eldership. Ambition is hidden within us. If the brothers and sisters say "amen" more loudly to someone else's prayer than to ours in a meeting, we may become jealous. We may be bothered, and after the meeting we may not be able to eat our meal happily. Even in marriage life there may be competition between the husband and wife. For a wife to question the headship of the husband offends him greatly. The husband may be bothered that everyone seems to listen to his wife more than to him, or that his children seem to agree with his wife more than with him. This consideration is related to ambition.

THE PROBLEM OF OPINION

The problem of opinion can be seen in Matthew 16:21-26: "From that time Jesus began to show to His disciples that He must go to Jerusalem and suffer many things from the elders and chief priests and scribes, and be killed, and be raised on the third day. And Peter, taking Him to him, began to rebuke Him, saying, God be merciful to You, Lord; this shall by no means happen to You! But He turned and said to Peter, Get behind Me, Satan! You are a stumbling block to Me; for you are not setting your mind on the things of God, but on the things of men. Then Jesus said to His disciples, If anyone desires to come after Me, let him deny himself, and take up his cross, and follow Me. For whoever desires to save his soul-life shall lose it; but whoever loses his soul-life for My sake shall find it. For what shall a man be profited if he should gain the whole world, but forfeit his soul-life? Or what shall a man give in exchange for his soul-life?" In this portion of the Word, we can see opinion (v. 22), Satan (v. 23), the self (v. 24), and the soul-life (vv. 25, 26). Peter's disposition is clearly seen in these verses. Although the word *disposition* is not mentioned here, it can be seen in the elements of opinion, the self, the soul-life, and Satan. Satan is in our opinion, and our opinion comes from our self. It is the product of our disposition. Without opinion, there would be no such thing as disposition. A person's disposition is seen in his opinion.

In marriage life the sin of ambition does not arise every day, but the problem of opinion may arise many times each day. Both brothers and sisters have their opinions. However, the sisters may express them more easily, while the brothers keep their opinions within them. The brothers' opinions may be even stronger than the sisters' opinions, but the brothers may not express them. When a brother is driving a car, his wife may express many opinions about the way to drive, but the husband may silently carry out his own opinion.

In the Lord's work, in the church life, and in the spiritual life, the greatest damaging factor is our opinion. For many years in the Lord's work I have seen the problem of opinion. Our usefulness before the Lord depends greatly on the matter of our opinion. If we are opinionated, we are through with the Lord's work. In the past, the brothers over me in the Lord's work used me more when I had no opinion. When I had an opinion, they could not use me. Since I came out of mainland China in 1949, a number of saints have spontaneously come under my direction in the Lord's work. How much they can be used also depends upon their opinion. The more opinionated one is, the less he can be used.

Those who go out in gospel teams to visit people may have experienced the problem of opinions. On the one hand, when I worked with the co-workers in mainland China, I did not have any opinion. On the other hand, I had to "swallow" my opinion. I realized that if I expressed my opinion, I would be finished with the work. I might as well go into the world to find a job because the co-workers would not be able to work with me. If I would have been opinionated, the brothers above me in the work would not have used me, and the brothers under me would not have worked with me.

Apparently, the Christian life is an individual matter. Nevertheless, how much we grow in life also depends upon our opinion. How much growth we have had since we were saved has depended upon how we have dealt with our opinion. Opinion is a great matter. It is within us like the marrow in our bones. If the Lord tells us to go see a certain sister, we may say that we are not ready. This is our opinion. In Matthew 16:21 the Lord Jesus told His disciples that He was about to be crucified. Peter began to rebuke Him and said, "God be merciful to You, Lord; this shall by no means happen to You" (v. 22). This was Peter's opinion. To the Lord, Peter was like a mask hiding the source of the opinion. The source was not Peter but Satan. The Lord turned to Peter and said, "Get behind Me, Satan!" (v. 23). Opinion is a great and terrible problem, frustrating the Lord's way, will, plan, and economy.

I have been in the church and the work in the Lord's recovery for fifty-seven years. During this time, I have seen a number of turmoils in the church. A turmoil is like a storm. Since the Lord's recovery came to this country over twenty-five years ago, we have had only two major "storms." The factors causing the storms were ambition and opinion. A typhoon is a storm which is associated with hot climates. An earthquake, on the other hand, comes from a build-up of pressure within the earth that has no outlet. The "heat" and "pressure" which cause the turmoils in the church life are ambition and opinion. However, we should not be bothered by the storms. No storm comes that will not go away quickly, and the bigger storms pass even more quickly. Even the storms in the church life soon pass away.

All the turmoils in the church life are the same in principle. They are caused by people who seek for position but are not useful because of their opinion. A certain person may desire to be an elder. This is ambition. However, he may be an opinionated person, unable to control his opinion. This opinion spoils him for the eldership. In 1933 Brother Nee asked me to remain in Shanghai to work with him. One of the brothers with us desired to be an elder in the church. He "hunted" for the eldership for many years. However, he was opinionated and not suitable for the Lord's work, and his opinionated talk often damaged the work. Eventually, he set up a meeting in his home and hired a traveling preacher who knew many of our teachings. Under the direction of this brother, the traveling preacher wrote a long article defaming Brother Nee. This storm came from one person with ambition who sought for the eldership but did not get it because he was spoiled by his opinion.

The "gopher" of ambition and the "creeping thing" of opinion always join together to cause turmoil. It is even the same in the national and international political situation. The troublemakers are the ambitious ones who did not get what they strived for because they were not useful. Whether or not we are useful in the hand of the Lord depends upon the matter of our opinion.

The world and sin may not frustrate us from the growth in our spiritual life, but the ever present obstacle and frustration to our growth in our spiritual life is our opinion. Sometimes we do not express our opinion, but it is still there. Opinion is the expression of our disposition, and our disposition is the greatest problem for our growth in the divine life. In the Far East and in America, I have come to know a number of saints. They are lovely, they are very much for the Lord, and they mean business with the Lord. However, after many years, they have had little growth in life. Their unique problem is their opinion.

Our disposition is our self. Every human being has a disposition. It is in us and it is us. Our disposition makes it hard for us to release our spirit. From 1942 to 1948 Brother Nee passed through a long turmoil in which he was prevented from ministering. After the turmoil passed, one of the first messages he gave was on the breaking of the outer man and the release of the spirit. From that time on, the center of Brother Nee's speaking was almost always on the breaking of the outer man. The breaking of the outer man is the breaking of our disposition. I am still learning the lesson of how to deal with my disposition. Brother Nee warned us that if we do not learn the lesson of the breaking of the outer man before we are fifty years old, we will have a difficult time in the church life. It is easier to deal with our disposition when we are young.

QUESTIONS AND ANSWERS

Question: How do we deal with our disposition? Should we pray concerning our disposition, or should we seek more experience of the Lord?

Answer: The Lord does not seem to answer this kind of prayer. Romans 8:13 says, "If by the Spirit you put to death the practices of the body, you will live." The practices of our body are part of our character. Habitually, we always do things a certain way. We have to put to death our habits by the indwelling Spirit. The only thing that can solve the problem of our disposition and character is the cross. We have to take the cross to put our disposition to death. We may be willing to put to death the members of our body in relation to sin. However, our body has many practices every day. All these practices are according to our habits, and they also must be put to death. We need to pay attention to the matter of opinion and always condemn our opinion.

A brother may come to us and say, "Let us go to visit people by knocking on their doors." If we have learned the lesson of putting our disposition to death, we will say, "Amen! Hallelujah!" However, we may feel that we have the right to express our opinion and that we should not follow this brother blindly. Only the death of the cross can deal with our disposition. Our old man, the "I," has been crucified with Christ (Rom. 6:6; Gal. 2:20). Therefore, we have to let our opinion, our disposition, remain on the cross. This is the breaking of the outer man.

Question: Since our opinion affects how useful we are and how well we can work with others, how can we fellowship and coordinate with one another in the work?

Answer: We must put our opinion aside. It is hard for Christians to discuss the Lord's work. It is even hard to talk about being in one accord. In February of 1986, about five hundred co-workers and elders came together for a conference. The subject of that conference was the one accord. Eventually, that conference became the source of a turmoil. When three gospel team members come together, if one would say something to maintain the one accord, he may offend the other two. Because the one accord is a difficult matter, many Christians are like politicians. They say they agree with something when actually they do not. It seems they do not have any opinion, but actually they have many opinions.

Question: What should we do if something comes out in our fellowship that we strongly feel is not right?

Answer: We must take the lead to be without an opinion. Let the others with whom we fellowship say what they will. We should simply say, "Amen! I will go along with you." Then the others will follow our example. If we argue and correct others, we will set up a model of arguing and correcting, and the others will also argue. If we have learned the lesson of dealing with opinions, we will be an example of a person with no opinion. Then the others with us will also learn the lesson of dealing with opinions.

Often when I propose something, the brothers with me will propose something different. When this happens, I quickly go along with them. On the other hand, when the brothers propose something, I do not like to say something different. I prefer to go along with them and say, "Very good. Let us do it." It is the matter of opinion, our disposition, that makes us stubborn. We do not like to be changed or corrected. We like to insist on our way. If we do not break through to have our way this time, we will try again the next time. If we are like this, the older brothers cannot use us, and the younger brothers will not work with us. As a result, we will become isolated and useless. We should always go along with the brothers, with no opinion, putting our disposition to death. Then we will be useful.

Question: When some come together to fellowship, they are passive because they do not want to express their opinion. Is it correct to speak our opinion as long as we do not hold on to it and are willing for it to be dropped?

Answer: This is not correct. If we mean business about dropping our opinion, we have to go along with others positively. We may say that we will not do anything because we do not want to have an opinion. However, if we would not go along with others positively, we are holding back and keeping our opinion. If a brother proposes that we arrange the chairs in the meeting hall in an unusual way, would we do it? We have to learn to go along with the brothers. If we go along, the one who made the proposal will learn that he was wrong. Then he will propose that the chairs be restored to their former order. Simply go along, and do not blame him. Eventually, we will find the right way to arrange the chairs.

Ambition plus opinion builds up enmity and makes enemies. When a married couple goes on a trip, they may not agree on which route to take. They may argue, become unhappy, and cancel the trip. Arguing over opinions can also take place in the church life. In a certain denomination, the leaders came together to talk about church affairs. Eventually, they became angry with one another, and one brother threw a Bible at another brother.

If the members of a gospel team argue about which neighborhood to go to, the team will be ruined. We must be released persons. Even a little arguing will bind everyone in the team. When someone proposes something, we should go along. Then, if what we are doing is wrong, it will be exposed. To do something wrong is much better than to argue.

Question: What is the difference between having fellowship with one another and voicing our opinion?

Answer: The purpose of fellowship is to gain the Lord's presence. If we each go our own way and take care of our own portion without fellowship, it will be hard for us to enjoy the Lord's presence. The more we walk, work, and do things together, the more we will have the Lord's presence.

Question: When I have opinions, I may not express them in order not to cause a problem, but I feel hypocritical in simply going along outwardly. Is it right to be political in order to keep a pleasant atmosphere?

Answer: To have an opinion yet pretend that we do not have one is hypocrisy. We should condemn this. We should condemn our opinion and learn to despise and deny it. To deny our opinion is to deny our self. When we come together with others, we must deny ourselves, have no opinion, and go along with whatever the others propose. This is not hypocrisy. When the members of a gospel team come together and no one has an opinion, this is the best time for the Lord to do something. They should pray, "Lord, lead us and guide us. We want to follow You." In this way, something of the Lord will come out.

Question: How can we distinguish opinion from the feeling that comes from the Lord's leading?

Answer: Many of the feelings which we think are the Lord's leading are actually our opinion. The accuracy of our feelings depends on the breaking of our outer man through the cross and on how much we die to ourselves.

Question: I have some feeling that every week we should spend some time to visit new people by knocking on their doors, in addition to our home meetings, in order to contact new and fresh people all the time. Would it be the expression of my opinion to present this to my gospel team?

Answer: To practice the new way to meet and serve, we must first go out to knock on doors to get people saved and baptized. When we go out, we should not bring too many under our care. Each team member should have three or four people under his care. If we do not have a sufficient number to take care of, then we should go out again to knock on doors. Eventually, we should stop knocking on doors and take care of our two to four new ones for a certain period of time. After this, we should continue to follow the way given in our messages on the practice of the new way. The result will be a much better situation in the church than what we have had in the past.

However, many saints may only halfway follow the way given in our messages. They may go to visit people by knocking on their doors, but not in the way proposed in our messages. This is opinion. Only a person who does not insist on his opinion would fully take the way proposed in our messages. Because we have opinions, the Lord is not able to move quickly. Until we drop our opinions and take what is proposed in our messages, we will not see much fruit. If we practice what is proposed in our present messages, we will see the results.

The church life is different from school. When we were in school, the teachers gave us assignments which we had to do. If we did not do them, we received a failing grade. However, in the church life we may speak a message many times, yet the hearers may still only follow halfway. This is opinion. In the work, in the church, in marriage life, in private life, and in our Christian life, the greatest and the most difficult frustration is our opinion.

receiving (half-way / fully take the way).
functioning (carrying out .

THE EXPERIENCE AND GROWTH IN LIFE

MESSAGE TWENTY-THREE

THE EXPERIENCE OF LIFE

(12)

Scripture Reading: Matt. 16:21-26

THE SELF, SOUL-LIFE, AND DISPOSITION IN MATTHEW 16

The words *disposition* and *character* are difficult to define even with the best dictionaries. It is also very difficult to illustrate disposition and character. However, several terms used in Matthew 16:21-26 imply the matter of disposition. These terms include the mind (v. 23), the self (v. 24), and the soul-life (vv. 25-26). Though Matthew 16 does not use the word *disposition,* the matter of disposition is certainly implied here through the use of these terms. In this short portion, Peter's disposition is exposed.

According to Matthew 16:21-26, when the Lord Jesus told the disciples that He was going to be crucified, Peter reacted and took the Lord aside to rebuke Him. The Lord responded by rebuking Peter. Peter was rebuked by the Lord because Satan had used Peter to oppose the things of the Lord. Peter was used by Satan because there was something in his disposition which gave Satan the ground to use him.

Disposition refers to something within us. Disposition is implied in the terms *mind, self,* and *soul-life.* Disposition includes all of these elements; thus to refer only to the self or soul-life is inadequate.

OTHER KEY WORDS RELATED TO DISPOSITION

There are four terms mentioned in the New Testament which are closely related to the matter of disposition: the old man in Romans 6:6, the "I" in Galatians 2:20, the soul-life in

Matthew 16:25-26, and the self in Matthew 16:24. In addition to these terms, according to our study and experiences of the spiritual things in the New Testament, we have also used the term *naturalness* in relation to the matter of disposition. The contents of these five terms all imply disposition. A person's disposition includes all of these items.

Our disposition is expressed in many forms. One type is that of the "hero." Brothers or sisters who have this type of disposition must do everything in an impressive, perfect, and complete way. If they are to speak, they must do it in an outstanding way, or they will not speak. They are also very strong and quick in doing things. Another type of disposition is that of the "non-hero." The "non-hero" does not do anything in a thorough or complete way. If he or she locks the door, it is only partially locked; if he or she cleans a room, the corners are left undone.

In Message Twenty-one, we pointed out that our disposition is what we are in our makeup by birth and that our character is the outward expression of our disposition. Disposition is what we are within, and character is what we express without. The reason we are silent or talkative is due to our disposition. At the start of our full-time training, some brothers and sisters spoke very often, but after some weeks passed, perhaps due to some word of correction regarding their speaking, they became very silent. Their outspokenness was related to their disposition, but their self-enforced silence is related to their character.

Slowness is a matter of disposition. We may do everything very slowly. If we are rebuked for our slowness, we may become offended and react by doing everything in an extremely fast manner. What we express in this change of our outward behavior is no longer our disposition but our character. Disposition by itself does not directly involve anything of sin. But once our disposition is expressed with a hurtful intention, that is sin. Thus, our disposition has little to do with sin directly, but our character has a great deal to do with sin.

When you live according to your disposition and are corrected by others, your character is expressed in the way you change your behavior. An illustration of this is when little boys are playing a game with a ball. One of the boys may have the ball, dribbling it very slowly, and a friend may rebuke him for being so slow, asking him to pass the ball. When the first boy passes the ball, he may do it in an excessively fast and rough manner, reacting to the rebuke of the other boy. This way of passing the ball expresses the character of the first boy and is something naughty and sinful.

DEALING WITH DISPOSITION AND CHARACTER

The Scriptural Basis
for Dealing with Our Disposition

While there are no verses in the New Testament which directly tell how to deal with the disposition, there are a number of verses which can be used. Since the disposition is implied in the "I," the old man, the soul, and the self, our dealing with these things includes our dealing with the disposition. In Galatians 2:20, the "I" has been crucified. This "I" implies the disposition. In the same way, when we deny the self (Matt. 16:24) and lose the soul-life (Matt. 16:25-26), the disposition is dealt with, because it is implied in these things.

The Scriptural Basis
for Dealing with Our Character

Dealing with our character is seen in Romans 8:13, which says, "For if you live according to flesh, you are about to die; but if by the Spirit you put to death the practices of the body, you will live." The practices of the body are actually our character. To deal with the practices of the body is to deal with our character.

Dealing with Our Disposition by Living
under the Cross

In order to deal with our disposition, we must realize that we have been crucified (Gal. 2:20; Rom. 6:6). From morning to evening, throughout the entire day, we must remember that we are people who have already been crucified. Because we have been crucified, we should not live according to our disposition. We should not live, act, or walk according to what we are naturally. To live in such a way is simply to live according to our disposition. The way to deal with our disposition is to realize and remember that we are crucified persons and remain under that realization throughout the day.

Dealing with Our Disposition
by Opposing Ourselves

Along with the realization that we are crucified, we have to oppose ourselves. To oppose ourselves is to oppose our disposition. If you realize that your disposition is to be quiet, as long as you remain quiet, you are simply living according to your disposition. But if you would oppose your quiet disposition, you must first realize that your natural person has been crucified and then remain under the killing of the cross. Then in the meetings you, opposing yourself, can exercise to speak something of the Lord to the saints.

DISPOSITION AND USEFULNESS

The thing which most damages our usefulness in the Christian life and church life is our living according to our disposition. I have been in the Lord's work for many years, and I have found that some brothers and sisters have a strong element in their disposition which hinders them from coordinating and cooperating with others. If certain brothers or sisters are assigned a certain work, no one else can be included with them to help in that work; they must do it exclusively. Such brothers or sisters are usually very capable, and they can also easily stir up trouble in the church life.

The Lord's work is a work of the Body and by the Body; therefore, coordination is desperately needed. The Apostle Paul was very capable, but he also needed a number of others to help him and coordinate with him. Even if you are one of the top ones, there is still the need of coordination. Even the Lord Jesus Himself needed to coordinate with others. Actually, most of us do not like to work with others. If we are lazy, careless persons, we may like others to labor for us. But if we are diligent persons, laboring all the time, we may not

like others to work with us, because whatever they do inter-
feres with what we are doing.

In our spiritual life, in our Christian life, in our church
life, and in the Lord's work, we must learn to be people who
are always opposing ourselves. As a person with a strong disposition, I can testify that I must constantly realize that my
disposition is crucified. In the past, my confession was almost
completely about my failure to live Christ. Today, very often
my confession to the Lord is concerning my disposition. We
must learn to live a life of opposing ourselves. To oppose ourselves is to oppose our disposition.

USEFULNESS AND CAPACITY

Both the good and bad dispositions destroy our usefulness
in the spiritual realm. Our usefulness firstly depends upon
our capacity. In Matthew 25:14-15 the lord delivered his possessions to his servants according to their natural ability.
Their natural ability equals their capacity. The Apostle Paul
was a very capable person with perhaps the largest capacity.
But if Paul had not opposed his disposition, his disposition
would have destroyed his usefulness. How much the Lord can
use you depends upon your capacity. But regardless of how
much capacity you have, as long as you go along with your
disposition, you are finished. Throughout church history,
there have been many very capable brothers, such as Peter,
Paul, Martin Luther, John Nelson Darby, and Watchman
Nee. The Lord used these brothers very much. I can testify
that Brother Nee was not only a capable person with a large
capacity but also a person who learned to always be against
himself.

CAPACITY AND AMBITION

The reason for much of the political turmoil in the world
and the present turmoil among us is because of two factors:
ambition together with a lack of capacity. Someone may have
the ambition to be the president of a country, but not have the
capacity to hold such an office. When such a person is frustrated from gaining the office of president, he may then cause
trouble. On the other hand, a person may be very capable, but

if he has ambition, his ambition will destroy his capacity, his usefulness.

Actually, ambition is a large element of our disposition. If a country is going to be a strong country, it must produce a number of capable persons, who have a large capacity. Yet these persons also must be against their dispositions, that is, against their ambition. A person who is capable and who is also against his or her ambition is the most useful person. If a country can produce twenty such persons in a generation, that country will be one of the top countries.

CAPACITY WITHOUT AMBITION RESULTING IN USEFULNESS

Capacity without ambition makes a person very useful. On the contrary, capacity with ambition damages a person's usefulness. Throughout history, the persons who have damaged entire countries the most have been people who were very capable but who were too ambitious. Hitler was an example of such a person. He had a very large capacity, but along with his capacity, he had a terrible ambition. His capacity with his damaging ambition is the reason that Hitler damaged mankind so much. Capacity is good, but ambition is terrible.

The principle is the same in the Lord's work. The most fearful thing in the Lord's work is a capable person with ambition. On the other hand, one who is capable and without ambition is very useful in the Lord's work. In my whole life, by His mercy, I met a person who was the best example of someone who was very capable but without ambition. That person was Brother Nee. I can testify from my conscience that he was not ambitious at all. His work was of the highest standard. He did such a work, yet he did not keep anything for himself.

In the church in Shanghai, another brother who was also very capable was Brother Yu, who was an eye specialist. He translated the mystical books by authors such as Madame Guyon and Brother Lawrence into Chinese. I can testify concerning him that he was also without any ambition. Brother Yu along with a few other brothers took the lead in the church in Shanghai and in the work, but there was never any problem with ambition among these brothers. As a result, the church was built up, and many saints were edified.

Capacity without ambition means capacity plus the cross. Everyone is ambitious. Ambition is the primary element of every fallen person's disposition. Even the lowest persons with a very low capacity are ambitious. In the church life, some are very capable and ambitious, and others are not very capable, but they also are ambitious. Yet both can cause a great deal of trouble in the church life. How marvelous it would be if everyone in the church life was against ambition. If we all could be helped to live a life against our disposition, our ambition would be killed, and there would be no problems in the church life. Once ambition is killed in the church life, the usefulness of everyone, including those of limited capacity, will come out. But when the disposition of the saints is not dealt with, ambition comes out, resulting in turmoil, the usefulness of the saints is annulled, and a great deal of devastation is brought in.

A WARNING CONCERNING OUR DISPOSITION

If all the saints, especially those who are being trained to serve the Lord full-time, kill their disposition, everything will be very good. Otherwise, each trained one becomes a potential problem to the church. If we pick up the training and practice it with our ambition and capacity, trouble will be the result. If each trainee does not kill his or her disposition, each one is a problem and will be a problem. How useful you will be to the Lord or how much trouble you will make to the church depends upon how much your disposition is killed. Therefore, dealing with the disposition is a crucial matter.

THE EXPERIENCE AND GROWTH IN LIFE

MESSAGE TWENTY-FOUR

THE GROWTH IN LIFE

(12)

Scripture Reading: Matt. 16:21-26

THE DISPOSITION

Our disposition is what we are by birth, our natural makeup. In our experience, our disposition is found in the "I," the old man, the self, and the soul-life. Although there are no verses in the New Testament that clearly define the disposition, its significance is implied in certain portions of the Word. Galatians 2:20 says, "I have been crucified with Christ, and it is no longer I who live, but Christ lives in me." In this verse, the disposition is implied by the old "I," which has been crucified with Christ. In Matthew 16:21-26 and Luke 9:22-25 the disposition is implied by the self (Matt. 16:24; Luke 9:23, 25) and the soul-life (Matt. 16:25-26; Luke 9:24). In Matthew 16:22 Peter rebuked the Lord Jesus according to his disposition. Peter's disposition was mainly expressed in his quickness and in his taking the lead to express himself. Peter, as the spokesman of the twelve disciples, took the lead to express himself on many occasions. None of the other disciples exceeded Peter in this matter. We each have our own disposition. According to our disposition, we also may be quick to express ourselves as Peter did. On the other hand, according to our disposition, we may be persons who rarely say something to express ourselves.

Our disposition is the most difficult part of our being to deal with, and often there is a particular part of our disposition that is the hardest to deal with. It seems that a mountain can be moved more easily than certain parts of our disposition. Our disposition is a part of our self. As Christians, we have to live Christ by rejecting our self. We must learn to act against our disposition.

Our Disposition, Our Growth in Life, and Our Usefulness in Service

According to my observation over many years, the real enemy of our growth in the divine life is our disposition. Our disposition is also the factor that spoils our usefulness in the hand of the Lord. Shortly after I was saved, I received the vision of the Lord's recovery through the writings of Brother Nee, and I left the denomination with which I was meeting. In 1932 the Lord raised up a church in my locality, and in 1934 I began to work with Brother Nee. Since that time, as one caring for the church and the work, I have had contact with many people and have come to know them. I have learned that many saints eventually stopped growing in the divine life and could make no further progress. For the first few years of their Christian life they grew in the divine life very quickly. Eventually, however, their growth stopped due to a particular, peculiar aspect of their disposition. They had given up the world and had sacrificed many things for the Lord. They also listened to the messages and loved them. However, a particular, peculiar aspect remained in their being. That part of their makeup became a stronghold that held them back from making progress in the growth in life. There is little possibility for such saints to progress. Some saints have not grown in life for fifty years.

I have also seen some very promising saints who loved the Lord, sacrificed for Him in many ways, received a high education, and had much experience in sufferings and in the human life. As a rule, such ones are very useful to the Lord. However, because of a particular, peculiar aspect of their makeup, their usefulness was annulled. They did not insist on holding onto this aspect of their being; it simply remained in them and spoiled and stopped their usefulness.

Our particular traits can be compared to the grain in a piece of wood. A carpenter prefers to use wood that has an even grain. If the carpenter finds a piece of wood with an irregular grain, he will not use it. A piece of wood may be of good quality, but if it has a knot or a burl, it cannot be sawed easily; it is not useful. The Christians who do not have any peculiarity, any peculiar traits, are the ones who grow the most and the fastest. Likewise, the brothers and sisters who are the most useful are the ones who do not have any peculiar traits. In the service, the ones who are the most useful are the ones who always reject and deny what they are.

I have been observing the situation in the church for many years. When I was with Brother Nee, I saw a number of cases of rebellion, and in Taiwan and the United States I have seen several such cases. If we would diagnose these cases of rebellion, we could see that the source of the rebellion was the disposition of the persons involved. With almost no exceptions, the cause of each person's involvement in rebellion was their peculiar traits. On the one hand, many of the dear saints who have been involved in a rebellion were very useful. On the other hand, there was a "burl" within them, causing something negative to grow and accumulate. The "burl" eventually annulled their usefulness and led to rebellion. Many other dear saints, however, have not rebelled, but they were more useful in former years than they are today. They have remained in the church, but their usefulness has been annulled by their disposition. In the Christian life and in the work, disposition is a great negative factor.

Our Disposition and Our Human Life

If we look back at our life, we can realize that many of our sufferings were caused by the peculiar traits in our disposition. Because of his disposition, a student may be frustrated from studying, and his professors may not care for him personally. As a result, he will not be able to make good grades. If that person's disposition could be changed, he would be able to make better grades. In a law court, a judge may be negatively influenced by a person's peculiar traits, causing that person not to receive a favorable judgment. Even in a family, one child may suffer more than the other children because of his disposition. An employer may realize that an employee has a peculiar trait, but because the company needs him, they will keep him on. However, when the company begins to lay off its workers, he may be the first one to go. We may also suffer in our own neighborhood because of our peculiar traits. We may love people and love to help people, but because of our peculiar traits, none of our neighbors may care for us.

The negative factor in our marriage life and family life is our disposition. Seemingly, the problems between parents and children are due to certain mistakes. However, mistakes are easy to deal with. Mistakes are like dust on a desk top that can be wiped away. The real cause of the problems between parents and children are the peculiar traits in their makeup. If either the parents' or the children's disposition would change, there would not be such problems. However, even the parents are not able to change themselves. Eventually, the problems accumulate. Year after year there is an accumulation of problems. This accumulation may be compared to the cause of earthquakes. An earthquake is caused by the gradual accumulation of pressure underneath the earth which finally breaks forth. Even though the parents and children love each other and live for each other for many years, the accumulation eventually may lead to a big problem.

Our peculiar traits also cause us to suffer in our marriage life. A husband and a wife may love each other, but after being married for several months, the wife may discover a "burl" in her husband. The real problem between husbands and wives is the particular and peculiar part of their makeup, their disposition. This is the factor that can make the husband and wife unhappy. A pleasant husband and a pleasant wife are those who have no peculiar traits. A wife's beauty does not make her pleasant for long. A brother may be charmed by a sister's beauty while they are dating and on their wedding day, but after they live together for a short time, he may realize that he married a beautiful sister who is very hard to deal with. From that time on, the peculiar traits will cause trouble between them. The husband and wife may love and appreciate each other, but the accumulation of problems produced by their peculiar traits may eventually lead to divorce. In the church life, the accumulation of problems over many years may lead to rebellion.

Dealing with Our Disposition

In the four Gospels, Peter's most difficult dealing before the Lord was related to his disposition. Even by the time of Galatians 2:11-21, Peter's disposition had not yet been thoroughly dealt with. Something troubling still remained within him. According to the record of the whole New Testament, however, Peter eventually broke through. In Galatians 2 Paul rebuked Peter to his face because Peter still lived in his disposition to some degree, but in 2 Peter 3:15-16 Peter highly commended Paul. If Peter had been still living in his disposition, he would not have made such a strong commendation of the one who rebuked him. Rebuking offends people, but Peter was not offended. This may indicate that the "burl," the troublemaking factor, had been removed from him.

By man's hand there is no way to remove the factor of the disposition, but in the Lord's hand there is a way. In Matthew 19:25 the disciples asked the Lord, "Who then can be saved?" The Lord replied, "With men this is impossible, but with God all things are possible" (Matt. 19:26). This word must have been fulfilled in Peter. In 2 Peter 1:5-11 Peter wrote concerning the development of what the Lord has given us by the growth in life unto the rich entrance into the eternal kingdom. Peter was able to write such a word because he had learned the spiritual lessons. The Lord broke through in him. It is impossible for us to break through the problem of our disposition, but it is possible for the Lord to do it.

In the first few years of our spiritual life, we may have grown quickly. However, our growth may have slowed down or even come to a standstill because of our disposition. We should be warned concerning our disposition. We must learn to take care of the "burl" in our makeup, our disposition. If we deal with the "burl," we will grow quickly and have a free way in our spiritual life without any hindrances to our growth in life. We will also become more useful to the Lord.

QUESTIONS AND ANSWERS

Question: Why does our disposition not frustrate r growth in life at the beginning of our spiritual life?

Answer: At the beginning of our spiritual life, our disposition was buried by our worldliness, weaknesses, and sins. We grew quickly by dealing with the world, our weak points, and our sins. After we dealt with these superficial, negative things, we reached a deeper problem. The deeper problem was what we are. In our being, there was a "burl." Our free way was cut off. We could not go on and became blocked in our spiritual life. Our disposition has become our problem. It hinders us from growing in life and from being used by the Lord, and it has made trouble for us, causing us to suffer.

THE EXPERIENCE AND GROWTH IN LIFE

MESSAGE TWENTY-FIVE

THE EXPERIENCE OF LIFE

(13)

Scripture Reading: 1 Cor. 7:10, 12, 25, 40; Gal. 2:20

FOUR CRUCIAL VERSES IN 1 CORINTHIANS 7

In this message we will consider the experience of Christ in 1 Corinthians 7. Brother Nee once said that the highest level of spirituality for the New Testament believers is revealed in 1 Corinthians 7. He considered that Paul's spirituality, as seen in this chapter, was on the highest peak, making Paul the most spiritual person. In 1 Corinthians 7, there are four crucial and very unique verses. In verse 10 Paul says, "But to the married I charge, not I but the Lord, a wife should not be separated from her husband." The phrase "not I but the Lord" is similar to Galatians 2:20 where Paul says, "It is no longer I who live, but Christ lives in me." The charge in this verse is a serious one since it concerns God's ordination of marriage, so Paul has the confidence to say, "not I but the Lord." But in verse 12 Paul says, "But to the rest I say, not the Lord, if any brother has an unbelieving wife and she consents to dwell with him, let him not leave her." In this verse Paul is bold to speak his own word to the Corinthians, yet what he spoke became a part of the divine revelation.

In verse 25 Paul says, "Now concerning virgins I have no commandment of the Lord, but I give my opinion as having received mercy of the Lord to be faithful." Paul gives his opinion concerning the important matter of virgins based upon his having received mercy of the Lord to be faithful. Paul seemed to say, "Up to this point, I have not received a commandment of the Lord, but I give you my opinion, my feeling, concerning the matter of virgins. I admit that what I have to say is my opinion, but my opinion has been constituted with the Lord's mercy, making me a faithful one."

In verse 40 Paul says, "But she is more blessed if she so remains, according to my opinion; but I think that I also have the Spirit of God." The word "opinion" in this verse may not seem to be so pleasant or sweet. When the Lord spoke, He did not have to qualify His word by saying that His word was His opinion. He simply spoke because as the Lord and Master, He is the "Boss." But Paul, as a servant of the Lord, must first qualify his word when he speaks his opinion. Many so-called spiritual men today do not speak in such a way. Rather, they usually speak by saying, "I assure you that this is the right way. What I say is of the Lord." Paul, however, did not speak in this way. He simply said what he thought according to his opinion. Yet in giving his opinion, he was not alone; he had the Spirit of God with him.

PAUL'S EXPERIENCE OF CHRIST IN 1 CORINTHIANS 7

Before he was saved, Saul of Tarsus persecuted the saints and devastated the church. After he was saved, he became a different person and began to speak for the Lord in the way revealed in the preceding verses. The Old Testament principle of speaking for God (prophesying) is, "Thus saith the Lord" (Isa. 10:24; 50:1; Jer. 2:2; Ezek. 2:4). But the New Testament principle of incarnation is, "I (the speaker) charge." The speaker and the Lord are one. When Paul spoke, you can say not only that he spoke but also that the Lord spoke. Paul and the Lord were one in the principle of incarnation.

INCARNATION AND
THE PRINCIPLE OF INCARNATION

Incarnation is God entering into man to mingle Himself with man, making Himself one with man. God was incarnated in the Man Jesus Christ. He is a wonderful person, a unique person, with two natures. He has the divine nature and the human nature, yet these two natures do not stand separately; they are mingled together. He is the unique God-man.

The two natures of Christ being mingled together can be illustrated by tea and water. Tea is composed of two elements:

tea and water. When we say that we are drinking tea, we actually are drinking tea and water. Therefore, we can say that we are drinking tea-water. God can be likened to tea, and man can be likened to water. As tea and water are mingled together to make tea-water, God and man were mingled together to make a God-man, the Lord Jesus. This God-man is the mingling of two elements, two natures, into one entity without a third nature being produced. In tea-water, the two elements of tea and water remain distinct but are not separate. They exist together in a mingled way. It is the same with the Lord Jesus Christ as the God-man with the two natures of divinity and humanity.

LIVING A LIFE OF COINHERENCE AND MINGLING VERSUS LIVING AN EXCHANGED LIFE

In theology the word *coinhere* has been used to describe how two things not only co-exist but also exist within one another. In John 14:10 the Lord said to the disciples, "Do you not believe that I am in the Father, and the Father is in Me?" And in John 15:4 the Lord said further, "Abide in Me and I in you. As the branch cannot bear fruit of itself...." Both of these passages indicate coinherence, which is the mutual indwelling and mingling of two elements for them to be one entity, and these two mingled elements are distinct but not separate.

The matter of coinherence is often missed by Christians in their reading of the New Testament. As a result, our relationship with the Lord is often misunderstood. Some have said that we as Christians live an exchanged life. According to this understanding, Christ replaces and discards our poor human life with His superior divine life. If we read Galatians 2:20 in a superficial way, we may be misled to think that the concept of exchange is spoken of in this verse. This is because Paul says that he was crucified with Christ, that he no longer lives, and that now Christ lives within him. Many Christians, in reading Galatians 2:20, have held and still hold such a concept. The biography of Hudson Taylor has helped many Christians over the years, but the writer of this biography, Hudson Taylor's daughter-in-law, Mrs. Howard Taylor, promoted the mistaken concept of an exchanged life.

The proper concept concerning our relationship with Christ is coinherence—Christ lives in us and we live in Christ (John 15:4-5). God in Christ put Himself into us (Col. 1:27; Rom. 8:10) through regeneration (John 1:12-13; 3:6), and then we were put into Christ through baptism (Rom. 6:3; Gal. 3:27; Matt. 28:19). We were not thrown away or discarded, but we were put into the Triune God (Matt. 28:19). Instead of being thrown away, we have been put into Christ. Christ is now within us, and we are in Christ. This is really wonderful!

THE LORD'S PRAYER IN JOHN 17
REVEALING THE COINHERING ONENESS

In John 15 the fact of our being in Christ and Christ being in us is clearly revealed (vv. 4-5). But in John 17 the Lord prayed for our realization of this fact (vv. 20-21). He prayed so that we would realize we are in Him like He is in the Father and He is in us like the Father is in Him. With the divine Trinity, there is such a wonderful coinhering oneness. This coinhering oneness has been duplicated by Christ with His believers. Today Christ is in His believers, causing His believers to be in Him. This is like the Father being in the Son, causing the Son to be in the Father. The prayer of Christ in John 17 is a revelation of such a coinhering oneness. According to John 15 and 17, our relationship with Christ is one of coinherence, not of exchange.

DEALING WITH OUR DISPOSITION
BY THE CROSS OF CHRIST

In the New Testament, the one with the strongest disposition was perhaps the Apostle Paul. His disposition inwardly was very strong, but his stature was probably small and thin. Although Paul's disposition was strong, in reading 1 Corinthians 7, you cannot see his strong disposition. Paul wrote to the believers in Corinth who were of the logical and philosophical Greek background. He wrote in a very logical manner, but you cannot discover a hint of his strong disposition. The person of Paul was there, but the "snake" of his disposition had been dealt with. In 1 Corinthians 7, the person who was Saul of Tarsus with the strong disposition had been dealt with, but the regenerated Paul remained. According to Paul's word in Galatians 2:20, he was crucified with Christ. His being crucified with Christ dealt with his disposition.

In Galatians 2:20, there is the old "I" and the new "I." The old "I" included the disposition of Saul of Tarsus. Although his disposition was crucified, Saul was not thrown away. On the contrary, through regeneration Saul of Tarsus was uplifted. As the sand on the seashore is sifted in order to find the precious things, Saul of Tarsus was sifted. All the negative and fallen things were put away, but the regenerated person of Saul was uplifted and purified. As saved sinners, our negative aspects have been put away, but our positive aspects are being uplifted. Through regeneration we have an uplifted humanity. This does not mean that we have exchanged our old humanity for a new humanity. We still have the humanity we received at birth, but before regeneration our humanity was old and of a low standard. After regeneration our humanity is being sifted, and through such a process it is being uplifted and purified. This uplifted and purified humanity is the new "I" in Galatians 2:20. Paul says, "And the life which I now live in the flesh I live in faith...." Paul lived by the life which is Christ Himself.

In 1 Corinthians 7, the person of Saul who became Paul still remained. Through the sifting process, Saul became Paul, a person who had been uplifted and purified with a high standard of humanity. Such a person is joined to the Lord and is one spirit with the Lord (1 Cor. 6:17). While Paul was writing 1 Corinthians 7, he was joined to the Lord as one spirit. Therefore, he could give a command saying, "I charge," and he could also say, "Not I but the Lord." He could say such things because he was one spirit with the Lord. His strong disposition had been sifted away through the cross of Christ, objectively in the fact of being crucified with Christ and subjectively in the experience of this fact. Paul experienced the subjective cross of Christ by experiencing the subjective Christ. Paul was a person who lived under the shadow of the cross all the time; thus, when he wrote 1 Corinthians 7, he was a regenerated, sifted, uplifted, and purified person who was joined to the Lord as one spirit.

THE PRINCIPLE OF INCARNATION
SEEN IN THE GRAFTED LIFE

Paul wrote 1 Corinthians 7 in the principle of incarnation. The principle of incarnation is that God enters into man and mingles Himself with man to make man one with Himself. Thus, God is in man and man is also in God. This can be illustrated by grafting. When two trees are grafted together, both trees must be cut. The cut in the first tree is an opening to receive the other tree. The second tree must also be cut in order to be put into the first tree. Then the two cuts are put together and the two trees begin to grow together. In order for us to be grafted into Christ, Christ and we must be cut. This cut was made at the cross of Christ. Christ as the good, cultivated olive tree (Rom. 11:17-18; John 15:1) was cut through His death on the cross. We also were cut by our crucifixion with Christ on the cross (Gal. 2:20). When we believed into Christ and were baptized into Him, we were grafted into Christ, the two cuts were put together, and we began to live together with Christ. There was no exchange of lives; rather, two lives were joined together and began to grow together organically (Rom. 6:4-5).

A stanza in a hymn written by A. B. Simpson (*Hymns,* #482) speaks of the matter of grafting:

> This the secret nature hideth,
> Harvest grows from buried grain;
> A poor tree with better grafted,
> Richer, sweeter life doth gain.

DEALING WITH THE DISPOSITION
THROUGH THE PROCESS OF SIFTING

In the grafted life on Christ's side, there is no need of sifting because there is nothing negative with Him. But on our side, we need a lot of sifting because we are full of negative things. After we were saved and came into the church life, we brought a number of negative things with us. These negative things can be considered as sand for sifting. All the sand must be sifted away. The trials we experience in the church life are used by the Lord to sift us. Wives, husbands, children, and even all the brothers and sisters in the church life are sifting means. In human life and in the church life, we all would prefer to have a peaceful life without any turmoil or storms. Many of the elders of the churches would certainly prefer a glorious church life without any troubles or problems. We may prefer such a church life, but often we have just the opposite. It is difficult to tell which is the best. When we get into eternity and look back, we may say that we had too little turmoil and too few problems that could have sifted us.

Paul's church life was often full of turmoil (2 Cor. 11:23-33). On Paul's journey from Caesarea to Rome in Acts 27—28, there were many storms and hardships. Brother Nee's life in China from the beginning of his ministry to the end of his life was full of turmoil. In the eighteen years that I was with him in the work, there was hardly ever a peaceful time. The last twenty years of his life, from 1952 to 1972, were spent in prison; those years in prison ended in his death.

Turmoil is a blessing because by it we are sifted. This sifting is related much more to our disposition than to our sins or mistakes. If by His mercy and grace, we all can pass through the sifting process, we will remain useful to the Lord. Our usefulness does not depend upon our good disposition by birth. Our usefulness is determined by how much we have been sifted. It is better to have a strong disposition which passes through the sifting process day by day and year after year than merely to have a good disposition. Paul was a person with a strong disposition who had passed through a long term of sifting through many storms; therefore, he could write a chapter such as 1 Corinthians 7.

SUMMARY AND CONCLUSION

First Corinthians 7 is the writing of a man, yet this composition became the divine revelation. He could say that his word was not the commandment of the Lord, but the word he gave became the divine revelation. At the end of this chapter, Paul concludes by saying that what he had given was according to his opinion and that he thought that he also had the Spirit of God. He not only had his opinion, but he also had the Spirit of God. These two things speak together in the mingled way: the Spirit of God speaks in his opinion, and his opinion expresses something with the Spirit of God. God mingled with man as one person with two natures, living together in one life and one living, is the experience of the grafted life in the principle of incarnation. This is the real dealing with the disposition.

THE EXPERIENCE AND GROWTH IN LIFE

MESSAGE TWENTY-SIX

THE EXPERIENCE OF LIFE

(14)

A WORD OF TESTIMONY
CONCERNING THE LORD'S CALL

In the summer of 1933, I was called by the Lord to serve full-time, yet I struggled with the Lord concerning this matter for about three weeks. Although I eventually turned in my resignation to my employer, I continued to have an inward struggle for some time. On the day I turned in my resignation, that same night after a prayer meeting, I talked to a leading brother and a leading sister concerning my decision to drop my job to serve the Lord. Although they both confirmed my decision, I still felt that I lacked the confirmation from the Lord. But as I went to the Lord later that evening, I was immediately rebuked by the Lord for my lack of faith in trusting Him. Eventually, through this experience, I became clear that the Lord really wanted me to drop my job. The next day confirmation came in the form of a letter of invitation from a group of Presbyterian believers in Manchuria. This invitation which was waiting for me at the post office had arrived on the day I resigned from my job. This was a real confirmation to me of the Lord's leading. Based upon this invitation, I went to my boss and asked him to allow me to go to Manchuria for a period of time and that when I came back, I would arrange everything with him concerning my job. He agreed.

In Manchuria I baptized about twenty believers, and those believers became the start of the church life in that region. This made me very happy. While I was in Manchuria, a letter came from my former employer in which he asked me to stay on at the company, and he also promised to increase my salary. It was also the policy of the company to give large bonuses to its employees at the end of the year. This coming bonus became a real temptation to me. I began to reason within myself, saying, "It is now September, and I would have only three months to go. Why not wait until the end of December to leave? Would three months make that much difference? If I wait until December, I could get that big bonus." Because of this kind of reasoning, I went back to Chefoo with some possibility to remain in the employment of that company until the first part of January. But when I returned home from Manchuria, a letter from Brother Watchman Nee, who was on the way back to China from England, was there for me. The letter contained only a short note saying, "Brother Witness, concerning your future, I feel that you should serve the Lord full-time. How do you feel about it? May the Lord lead you." I was very touched by this short letter because I knew that it was not Brother Nee's practice to write such notes to anyone. I was touched even further when I saw that the date of his letter corresponded almost exactly with the time of my struggle. This meant that as I was struggling, he somehow came to know about it. That surprised me very much. This letter from Brother Nee strongly countered the letter from my employer and greatly inspired and strengthened me. Eventually, I decided to go to the office and hand over my job to another person as soon as possible. I also resolved to go to Brother Nee and find out how and where he wrote that letter to me. After I left the job, I went to Shanghai in the fall of 1933 to see Brother Nee and ask him why he had written that note to me. He answered that one day while he was sailing from England to China on the Mediterranean Sea, as he was with the Lord, the Lord gave him the feeling that he should write a note to me. He then wrote a short note, sent it to the bookroom in Shanghai, and the bookroom then forwarded the letter to my home in Chefoo.

I was very inspired by his letter because I knew that his sending of the letter was not a coincidence; it must have been something of the Lord. I also was very impressed with Brother Nee, because this demonstrated that he was a man very much with the Lord. Otherwise, how could he have had such a feeling to write a note to me in China while he was far away on a trip from England to China? He was a man with the Lord; therefore, even to this very day I can declare that I completely trusted him. Brother Nee was also not the kind of person who always told people what to do. Many times brothers would come to him and ask him whether or not he felt that they should go to a certain place to labor or not. Often Brother Nee would not answer them because he refused to be in the principle of the Old Testament prophet. He taught that in the Old Testament, if one needed to know something concerning God, he would go to a prophet, such as Elijah, but in the New Testament, the believers have the anointing (1 John 2:20, 27). Therefore, we have no need for anyone to teach us. He practiced this very strongly, but in this instance, he wrote such a note to me. This confirmed to me that this was really something of the Lord.

LEARNING TO BE OCCUPIED
WITH THE LORD'S CURRENT SPEAKING

In the spring of 1934, Brother Nee gave a series of messages concerning the centrality and universality of Christ. Within that same period of time, he also spoke concerning the overcomers, using Abraham as an illustration. At that time, the words *centrality* and *universality* were very new to me, and I was very impressed as Brother Nee shared concerning this matter. In those messages, which were printed in his book *The Present Testimony,* Brother Nee spoke concerning Christ being the Firstborn of all creation (Col. 1:15). He shared that Christ is not only the Creator, but as the Firstborn of all creation, He is also a creature. As the Creator He is God, and as our Savior in His humanity with the human nature, He is a creature. He left the position of God to come to take the position of a man.

Brother Nee spoke this message in 1934, and it was recently translated into English. In the English translation, however, the word *position* was changed to *place.* It says that Christ as God left the *place* of God and came to the *place* of man. While the words *position* and *place* are close in meaning, there is an important difference. Let me illustrate. To say that the queen of England left her position in England to take the position of a civilian in Hong Kong means that the queen of England became a civilian. But to say that the queen of England left the place of the queen to come to the place of a civilian in Hong Kong only means that her place, her location, not her position of being a queen, has changed. In other words, the queen of England left her place in England to visit the civilian place of Hong Kong, but she did not become a civilian. But in incarnation Christ not only came to the place of man, but also came to the position of man (Phil. 2:5-7). This indicates that a big change occurred. In other words, Christ, who is God the Creator, became a creature.

Those messages given by Brother Nee impressed me so much that my mind was occupied with them day and night for a long time. After that conference, I remained in Shanghai for several months, and then I returned to Chefoo. In Chefoo I immediately called a conference and shared what Brother Nee had spoken in the conference in Shanghai nearly word for word. Since you are trainees in this training, I hope and expect that you also will eventually be able to do the same, especially with the recent messages of the Thanksgiving conference given in Anaheim. These messages tell us what the church is intrinsically. (See *The Organic Building Up of the Church as the Body of Christ to Be the Organism of the Processed and Dispensing Triune God* published by Living Stream Ministry.)

THE INTRINSIC NATURE OF THE CHURCH AND THE INTRINSIC FACTOR OF THE WINDS OF TEACHING

The church has four intrinsic matters on the positive side: its intrinsic essence, its intrinsic growth, its intrinsic building up, and its intrinsic fellowship. The one intrinsic matter on the negative side related to the church is the intrinsic factor of the winds of teaching.

The church's intrinsic essence, intrinsic growth, intrinsic building up, and intrinsic fellowship are organic. The church is built up intrinsically, organically. To be built up organically is to grow in life intrinsically, that is, to grow in the Triune

God who has been processed and who is now dispensing Himself into us as our life and life supply. As we are growing, we are built up. The church, which is the Body of Christ and the house of God, is the organism of the processed and dispensing Triune God seen as the universal vine tree in John 15.

Many Christians do not understand or consider the church as something intrinsic. Rather, they consider the church in terms of outward and even physical things. This outward understanding regarding the church is the factor of the turmoil among the churches. If we do not know the intrinsic essence, intrinsic growth, intrinsic building up, and intrinsic fellowship of the church, we can be sifted. Without the proper view of the church according to these four intrinsic matters, we all can be tossed and carried about by the winds of teaching. But if we know these four intrinsic matters, we will never be carried away or shaken. This is the reason that I felt compelled to give the messages in the recent Thanksgiving conference in Anaheim.

Positively, the essence, growth, building up, and fellowship of the church are all intrinsic. Negatively, the winds of teaching also have an intrinsic factor—the sleight of men (Eph. 4:14). By looking at the church outwardly, you cannot know what the church is. In order to know what the church is, you must get into the intrinsic element of the church. It is the same regarding the turmoil and opposition. On the surface, it is not so easy to discern the winds of teaching, but underneath the surface, the intrinsic factor of the winds of teaching is the sleight of men in craftiness with a view to a system of error. The sleight, the craftiness, is of men but the system is of Satan. Satan has systematized some of the teachings which seem to be good and scriptural, but these teachings have a view to spoil and destroy the faith of the saints, to devastate and pull down the building of the church, and to scatter the saints. In the present turmoil, to ask who is right or wrong is not the real issue. You must ask whether or not the messages given by certain opposing ones have strengthened the saints' faith and their growth in life. Have these messages really built up the Body of Christ?

The winds of teaching cause your faith to be weakened

and raise doubts about the church life and the Lord's recovery. Although many saints remain positive, these doubts and suspicions within them have become a factor which weakens and even shakes their faith. Some have been so influenced by the winds of teaching that they have withdrawn from the meeting life and have fallen into worldly, sinful activities. The winds of teaching in the sleight of men are very subtle and issue in devastation and damage to the church.

A TESTIMONY CONCERNING
THE CHURCH LIFE IN CHINA

The problems in the church life and among the churches come from something which is not intrinsic or organic, that is, from something which is not the processed and dispensing Triune God. When I trace our history in mainland China from 1922 to 1949, I have a very deep impression concerning the church in Shanghai. Among a group of five saints (three brothers and two sisters) who formed the crucial center of the church, there was never any kind of dissension, opinion, or ambition. Of course, in those years turmoil came in on some occasions, but it was always outside of these five. The principle we kept was to have nothing for ourselves. We did not labor for anything for ourselves; we just labored for the Lord's recovery. At the same time, we lived in the way of the intrinsic essence of the church. There was a strong coordination among us five brothers and sisters, and each of the brothers and sisters knew and remained within his or her limit or sphere. We also had full and complete trust in one another.

Brother Nee went to Hong Kong in 1950 and brought in a great revival to the church there. He then asked me to go there to arrange all the services of the co-workers, the elders, and the deacons. He also asked a small group of saints who were responsible for purchasing the land for the church meeting hall to do whatever I said concerning the purchase of the land. Again, this is the way we practiced the church life; everyone stayed within his own limit, and everyone knew where he was. I hope that we all would learn to serve the Lord in such an intrinsic way.

THE EXPERIENCE AND GROWTH IN LIFE

MESSAGE TWENTY-SEVEN

THE GROWTH IN LIFE

(13)

In previous messages we have seen that our disposition is our inward being, what we are inwardly, and our character is the outward expression of what we are inwardly. In a recent conference we saw four intrinsic matters of the church—its intrinsic essence, intrinsic growth, intrinsic building up, and intrinsic fellowship (see *The Organic Building Up of the Church as the Body of Christ to Be the Organism of the Processed and Dispensing Triune God* published by Living Stream Ministry). These four intrinsic matters are versus our disposition and character. They are versus our inward being and our outward expression. Without our inward being and our outward expression, there is nothing left in the church but God as the intrinsic element.

THE PROCESSED AND DISPENSING TRIUNE GOD BEING THE INTRINSIC ESSENCE, THE INTRINSIC GROWTH, THE INTRINSIC BUILDING UP, AND THE INTRINSIC FELLOWSHIP OF THE CHURCH

The four intrinsic matters of the church are God Himself. The intrinsic essence of the church is the divine life, and the divine life is God Himself. God is the intrinsic essence, the intrinsic growth, the intrinsic building up, and the intrinsic fellowship of the church. The intrinsic element of the church is simply God. This God is not the "raw" God, but the processed and now-dispensing Triune God who is embodied in Jesus Christ (Col. 2:9). God, who is the intrinsic element of the church, is Christ. Christ is the Head of the church (Eph. 1:22), the universal new man, and Christ is also the Body (1 Cor. 12:12; Col. 3:11). First Corinthians 12:12 says,

"For even as the body is one and has many members, but all the members of the body being many are one body, so also is the Christ." Christ is not only the Head but also the Body. Therefore, Christ as the embodiment of the processed and now-dispensing Triune God is the totality of the church.

Colossians 3:11 says, "Where there cannot be Greek and Jew, circumcision and uncircumcision, barbarian, Scythian, slave, freeman, but Christ is all and in all." Whatever is in the new man is Christ. In the new man there is no Greek, no Jew, no barbarian, no Scythian, no slave, and no freeman, but Christ is all. Christ is you and Christ is me. Christ is everything. In the new man Christ is all, and He is also in all. In Colossians 3:11 "all" refers to all the members who comprise the new man. All the members are Christ. None of the members are Chinese, none are British, none are black or white, and none are male or female. If verse 11 ended with "Christ is all," we might feel that Christ has replaced the members in the church. However, Paul added, "and in all." All the members are still in the church, but Christ is in all the members, and Christ even is all the members. The all-inclusive Christ is the church as a corporate entity because the intrinsic essence, intrinsic growth, intrinsic building up, and intrinsic fellowship of the church are the dispensing, processed Triune God who is embodied in Christ.

Christ is the embodiment of God. He is the complete God in His divine Trinity, and He is also a perfect man. Through His death and resurrection, Christ, who is the complete God and the perfect Man, became the Spirit (1 Cor. 15:45b; 2 Cor. 3:17). This very all-inclusive Spirit is the consummation of the Triune God. In eternity past the Triune God was not consummated, but by passing through the processes of incarnation, human living, the all-inclusive death, and resurrection, He was consummated to be the all-inclusive Spirit. Revelation 22:17 says, "And the Spirit and the bride say, Come!" The Bible ends with the divine, all-inclusive title—"the Spirit."

Christ is the embodiment of the Triune God, and the Spirit is the realization of Christ. Ephesians 4:4 says there is "one Body and one Spirit." This verse indicates that the Spirit and the Body are not two entities but one. The essence, growth, building up, and fellowship of the church are the processed and now-dispensing Triune God who is embodied in Christ, who is realized as the all-inclusive Spirit, the consummation of the processed Triune God.

THE BUILDING UP OF THE CHURCH THROUGH THE PURGING OF OUR DISPOSITION

Originally in God's creation there was only one man, Adam. Eve was not present in God's original creation. God took one of Adam's ribs and built it into a woman to be Adam's counterpart (Gen. 2:21-22). As Adam's counterpart Eve was his mate to match him. No other creature could be a mate to man to match him. God only needed a short time to build Adam's rib into Eve, but to build the believers into the church He has needed almost two thousand years. God has been building and is still building, and the building up of the church has required a long period of time.

Because the building has lasted for so long, the believers, who are the building materials, have had the opportunity to fight with each other and create turmoils in the process of its being built up. All these turmoils are for the building up of the church. The building up of a woman from Adam's rib was a type. The fulfillment of the type is the building up of the church, and the building of the church has passed through many turmoils. The turmoils in the church have been siftings. In Paul's time there was a sifting. Paul said, "All who are in Asia turned away from me" (2 Tim. 1:15). The churches in Asia forsook his ministry. However, this does not mean that no one in Asia remained faithful to the Lord's ministry. In Revelation 1 and 2, the seven churches in Asia were still remaining under the Lord's ministry. The turmoil portrayed in Numbers 16 was also a sifting. In Numbers 16 Korah and all his household were swallowed up by the earth (v. 32). However, certain Psalms were written by the descendants of Korah (Psa. 42; 44—49; 84—85; 87—88). There were still some left of Korah's family who became holy people and psalmists.

Those who cause the turmoils may not want to do so. However, their disposition causes them to do it. They may not be happy to make trouble, but they cannot help it. In the same way, we may not like to lose our temper with our husband or wife. When we lose our temper, we eventually regret it and may resolve never to do it again. However, after half an hour we may lose our temper once more because it is our disposition to do so. On the other hand, we may have been born with another kind of disposition. We may be those who can be very mad inwardly but are able to "swallow" our anger and not express it. We may be well-spoken of for our behavior, but within we are the same as those who lose their temper. Moreover, because of our disposition, it is difficult for us to be angry in a proper way as the Lord Jesus was with the money-changers in the temple (John 2:14-17). We live too much by our disposition in the church life. Therefore, the church is not purely and absolutely a constitution of God, Christ, and the Spirit.

No one cares for turmoils. According to our feeling, they are not good. However, the turmoils are necessary to deal with our disposition. Apparently, our disposition is a part of us that nothing can break and nothing can change. For us to have a dispositional change is like changing our very bone structure. Therefore, because of our disposition, the turmoils, in a sense, are needed for the building up of the church. In the past, certain saints were strongly in their disposition. However, they have suffered much because of the turmoils and have cried to the Lord. Their tears have been the best "detergent" to wash away their disposition. Today they are less in their disposition than they were before.

When we first came into the recovery, we thought the church was marvelous. That was the time of our "honeymoon." We may have expected that the honeymoon would last for our whole life. Eventually, however, the honeymoon became a "vinegar" moon. We may have asked ourselves, "Is this the wonderful church life?" Quite often the turmoils in the church life are like vinegar to us. The wonderful church life is a life not only with "honey" but also and more often with "vinegar." Many times it seems that this "vinegar" is everywhere in the church life. However, at other times there is a sweetness in the church life. The Lord is the best Physician. He knows how much "honey" and how much "vinegar" to prescribe for us. I recently had a skin problem, and the dermatologist told me to wash the affected area with vinegar water twice a day. The vinegar was effective in killing the germs. Eventually, because of the purging through the turmoils in the church life, which are like the vinegar, the Lord will declare that the "germs" in the church have been washed away.

OUR GROWTH IN LIFE
BY THE GROWTH OF GOD IN US

Now we want to go on to see that the building up of the church as the Body of Christ is by our growth in life, and our growth in life is by the growth of God in us. Colossians 2:19 says that all the Body grows with the growth of God. This means that our growth in the divine life needs God growing in us. When God grows in us, we grow with the growth of God.

This is quite deep and very mysterious. We may wonder how God could grow, but Colossians 2:19 tells us that if we are going to grow, we have to grow with some growth. We grow with God's growth. We can grow only with the growth of God. God is perfect and complete, so how can One who is perfect and complete grow? Growth is for maturity, but we know that God is ancient. He is not old, but He is ancient. The Old Testament calls Him "the Ancient of days" (Dan. 7:9, 13, 22). Does such an ancient One need to grow? The answer is this: in Himself God does not grow, but in you and me, He needs to grow.

God is in us, but how much is God in us? We Christians are the children of God, and we have God in us. God and we are mingled together as one person, but we have to check our real situation. Is there more of us and less of God, or more of God and less of us? We may declare that we have God and that God and we are one, but what about the fact of our case presently? Many of us have to admit that with us there is more of us and less of God.

We are more and God is less because we do not give Him the room in us. We do not give Him the cooperation. To give Him the room within us is to let Him grow. Any organic matter needs room to grow properly. In Matthew 13 the seed typifies the word with the divine life in it (vv. 3-23). This seed has been sown into our heart. It needs the adequate room to grow properly and fully. According to Matthew 13 in some cases the seed can hardly grow because many things in our heart leave no room for it to grow. There are many things other than God that occupy our heart. The Lord tells us that the thorns are the anxiety of the age and the deceitfulness of riches that choke the word (v. 22). All things other than God are choking things. These things choke the divine life, which is God, within us. Because of the occupying things in our heart, the seed of life within us does not have the room; it does not have the possibility to grow. In order for us to grow with the growth of God, we have to give God the room within us.

In every meeting we attend, we should give God the room within us. We should cooperate with Him. The Christian meeting is a realm for God to speak. If God cannot speak, He cannot gain anything. Most of the human race will not allow God to speak. God saves people and gathers them together in meetings so that He can speak in their speaking. Who will let God speak on this earth? God saves, rescues, separates us from the world, and gathers us together so that He can speak, but He cannot speak by Himself. In the New Testament age, God does everything in the principle of incarnation. He does not do anything by Himself alone. He always does things with man, in man, and through man by being one with man and by man being one with Him. For Him to speak today, He cannot speak by Himself. He has to speak through us.

God desires to speak, but do we speak? The practice of Christianity is that of one man speaking and the rest listening. Because not many of the Lord's children will speak, some professionals are trained to speak for the congregation. Surely God does not like this, so we are trying our best to put this practice aside and give God the opportunity to speak. God is in us, and He wants to speak. He wants us to speak so that He may speak in our speaking. But why do we not speak? We do not speak because with us there is too much of us and very little of the Triune God. If we cooperate with God to speak, He will gain the room within us to grow.

Many times and in many things, we do not give God the room in us. He is waiting within us for the opportunity to grow. He wants to grow in us. We need to give Him the room within us all the time. When we give Him the room within us, He grows, and His growth within us becomes our growth. Today within many Christians there is hardly any room for the indwelling God to grow. Even within us, according to my realization, there is not much room for Him to grow. On the Lord's Day morning, many of us come to the meeting and do not speak. God is in us, but we would not give Him room to grow. We can give Him a little bit of room by speaking. We need to speak for the Lord and speak the Lord forth. The more we speak, the more we will have to speak. The more we speak, the more we will be able to speak. The more we speak, the more we will learn how to speak. And the more we speak, the more we receive God's supply. The more we speak, the more we give God the room within us. Then He grows in us.

The reason we have endeavored and paid such a great price to change our way from one man speaking to all speaking is so that God may grow within us. The principle of letting God grow is not only in speaking in the meetings but also in all things in our daily life. In John 3:30, John the Baptist said, "He must increase, but I must decrease." This is God's way. He increases, and we decrease. The word *increase* and the word *grow* are the same word in Greek. To grow is to increase. We must let God grow, which means that we must give Him the room within us to increase. Then He has the way to grow in us in everything.

THE EXPERIENCE AND GROWTH IN LIFE

MESSAGE TWENTY-EIGHT

THE EXPERIENCE OF LIFE

(15)

Scripture Reading: Phil. 4:8   Phil 2-3-8

THE REST OF THE APOSTLE'S TEACHING CONCERNING LIVING CHRIST

Paul's teaching in the book of Philippians is concerning our living of Christ. After much teaching concerning the main aspect of his subject, in 4:8 he says, "For the rest, brothers, whatever is true, whatever is honorable, whatever is righteous, whatever is pure, whatever is lovely, whatever is well spoken of, if there is any virtue and if any praise, take account of these things." The phrase "for the rest" indicates that, though Paul has already written nearly four chapters, he still has more to say. He is still burdened to speak something further, but he does not have the time or the convenient way to finish his speaking, so he says, "For the rest." The other items he mentions in verse 8 are simply the outline of his further word. He does not give very many details, but he gives an outline comprising eight points. These points include: whatever is true, whatever is honorable, whatever is righteous, whatever is pure, whatever is lovely, whatever is well spoken of, any virtue, and any praise.

BEING TRUE, HONORABLE, RIGHTEOUS, PURE, AND LOVELY

First, you must be a true person involved with true things. Then, you must be a person who deals with honorable things, not touching anything dishonorable. You also must be a person who is right in every way with God and with man. You also must be a person who is pure, only touching pure things. With the people of God, purity means much more than it does to the unbelievers. To the unbelievers, whether something is pure or not is of little concern. But God's people must be pure in every way. As a child of God, you also must be lovely. This does not mean that you must be beautiful in outward appearance. Rather, it means that all the things you touch should be lovely. As a person you may be lovely, but the things you touch daily may not be so lovely. In the world, there are many lovely persons, but the clothing they wear and the places they go are absolutely not lovely.

BEING WELL SPOKEN OF

As Christians we also must be well spoken of. In Ephesians 1:3 the word "blessed" means to be well spoken of. God speaks well of us having blessed us with every spiritual blessing in the heavenlies in Christ. But the Devil, Satan, would never speak well of us. So, we must realize that to be well-spoken of is not easy. In Matthew 5:11 the Lord Jesus said that the persecutors would say every evil thing against the believers, lying. These evil things that are spoken about the believers are fabricated things. These fabricated things always have a little bit of truth in them. Though we may not have a good name because we are evil spoken of by our opposers and persecutors, we must try our best to touch only the things which can be well spoken of.

VIRTUE AND PRAISE

At the end of Philippians 4:8, Paul concludes with two items that sum up the points mentioned in the earlier part of the verse. These two items are virtue and praise. The phrase "if there is any virtue and if any praise" is difficult to understand. The word "praise" here does not refer to our praise of God. Rather, it refers to others' praise toward us concerning the things we do which are worthy of praise. The word "virtue" in English usage denotes the inner energy to do good things. In Luke 8:44-46 (KJV) when the woman touched the border of the Lord's garment, virtue went out from Him to heal her. This virtue was the power or strength to do good. But in Philippians 4:8, the meaning of virtue is different. Virtue here means excellent behavior or conduct. You may have good conduct, but unless it is the best, it cannot be considered virtue. Virtue is conduct on the highest level. If you have this kind of excellent conduct, whatever you do will be praised by others. First, there is excellent conduct or virtue, then there is praise by others.

If you are a person with all of these eight items, you are a person with good character, a person with excellent characteristics. Each of the items mentioned here is a characteristic, and these characteristics are your very expression. Your expression to people is your character. Character is your disposition expressed in an outward form. Inwardly, you have your disposition, and outwardly, you have your character.

THE RELATIONSHIP BETWEEN NATURE AND HABIT

Many elements of our character are often expressed unconsciously by our nature and habit. Character is constituted with thirty percent nature by birth and seventy percent habit formed by the daily life. Our character is expressed in many characteristics. These characteristics are built up with thirty percent of our nature and seventy percent of our habit. You may have been born a slow person. If you were under strict parents and teachers who would not allow you to be slow, but compelled you to be quick, it would change, to some extent, the slowness you received by birth. If, on the other hand, you were born slow and lived with parents who were also slow, then a habit of being slow would have been built up within you. The slowness you received by birth would be joined to a habit of slowness to form a character with this terrible characteristic.

LEARNING TO BUILD UP A DIFFERENT CHARACTER

The New Testament tells us that to follow the Lord we must learn to deny ourselves. Yet, we must ask, what is the self? The self within is our disposition, and the self expressed is our character. We often say that young boys are very stubborn and young girls are not. A father may be very stri ᵗⁿ dealing with his son when he does something wrong. But his son will not do what he tells him to do, even after tʰ agrees with his father to do it. This exposes the youn stubborn character. If he is very stubborn with his father, he may be even more stubborn as a brother in the church life or when he has his own family.

Males usually have a particular characteristic of being stubborn in an apparent way, while females do not seem to be stubborn at all. Actually, both males and females are stubborn because they both are descendants of Adam. Even though males and females are the same in some aspects of character, there are some differences. Females or sisters, being the weaker vessels (1 Pet. 3:7), have a number of small weak points. One of the most apparent weak points is the matter of shedding tears. Females may be weak by nature, but they must exercise not to form a habit of shedding tears. Once such a habit is developed, it becomes a strong element in their character. This character is just the self. The Lord said in Matthew 16:24 that anyone who desires to come after Him must deny himself. The self that must be denied in the case of the sisters is the dropping of tears.

Brothers, however, have the opposite problem of not shedding tears. In Acts 20 Paul testified that he served the Lord and admonished the saints with tears (vv. 19, 31). Many times after reading this I have rebuked myself for not shedding tears. I have gotten into the habit that when tears come, I call them back so that they only fall inside of me and not outside. But sometimes, to follow the Lord, we must be able to shed tears. Brothers must learn to be against themselves to shed tears, and sisters must learn to be against themselves not to shed tears.

CHRISTIANS HAVING THE HIGHEST CHARACTER

As Christians we are people on the highest level. Whether we are rich or poor, highly educated or uneducated, we are people of a high standard. We may have a low position in society, but whatever we do, even if it is to sweep the street, it should be done according to a high standard. Our character must be very high. For example, we may prefer quickness to slowness. But often, our quickness is too wild without any standard. Even quickness must be the proper quickness according to a high standard. The way we take care of our hair should also be of a high standard, even honorably.

The eight items mentioned in Philippians 4:8 are items we must pick up to build up our character. We must be people with a character which is true in every way, honorable in everything, righteous, pure in every aspect, lovely, and well-spoken of. Though we cannot avoid being belittled, smeared, and damaged by our persecutors, we do have a certain kind of character. This character is something which has been built up and constituted within our being over many years. As human beings, we all have certain characteristics which are points of our character. Therefore, if we hear an accusation against someone we have known for a number of years, we do not receive it. The reason for this is that we know the character of that person. This person's character has certain characteristics which do not correspond to the accusation.

DEVELOPING CHARACTER
BY CULTIVATING PROPER HABITS

Young people should try their best to pick up good habits. One such habit is making your bed in the morning. If I want to find out about a young man's character, the first thing I would look at is his bed. This is a small thing, but what we are is more easily expressed in small things than in big things. In big things, we can perform or act as actors, but in small things, we are really genuine, expressing what we really are. I recommend the book *Character* to you that it may be a help in developing your character. The first three points of character presented in this book are genuineness, exactness, and strictness. To be genuine is to be what you are without any pretension. To be exact is to be accurate, without understatement or exaggeration. In married life, many separations and divorces are due to carelessness and inaccuracies. In the church life, inaccuracies can cause a lot of trouble. We must practice to build up our character by learning to be genuine, exact, and strict.

By practicing, we build up a habit. For example, s
dust the middle of a piece of furniture, neglecting tl
But others dust the entire piece of furniture th

This is by habit. We must build up a habit of doing things thoroughly. We also should practice to be accurate. A person who does not practice to be accurate cannot rightly understand the Bible. If you practice to be accurate, when you read the Bible, you will read it accurately, because this is your habit. For example, 1 Corinthians 14:23, a verse which is very familiar to us, says, "If therefore the whole church comes together in one place." The first two words are neglected by most readers. The word "therefore" simply indicates a continuation of the foregoing verse. But the word "if" indicates a great deal more. If the church comes together regularly, there is no need to say, "If the church comes together." "If" indicates that the whole church does not come together regularly. Our practice corresponds to this verse. The New Testament way of practicing the church meetings was to mainly meet in the homes. Sometimes, the whole church came together, so "if" is used. This is an example of accuracy and strictness. If by practice you have been built up as a strict and accurate person, you will pay attention to each word of the Bible.

QUESTIONS AND ANSWERS

Question: Should we use our natural effort to build up our character?

Answer: No, we should not. As Christians seeking after the Lord, we do not need to do anything by our own effort. We should always do things first by prayer. This is the reason that the Bible charges us to pray unceasingly (1 Thes. 5:17). We should praise the Lord and tell Him that we are weak and unable to do what we should do. Then, after some prayer, we should exercise to trust in the Lord and look unto Him daily. If we are concerned about our character, we should pray, trust in the Lord, and look unto Him. We look unto Him to help us build up our character and to rescue us from our old habit. This is what is meant by endeavoring. In Colossians 1:29, Paul said that he struggled. It seems that it is we who are struggling, but actually, we trust the Lord to do things. When we say that we must endeavor to do things, this does not mean that we do things with our own effort like Olympic athletes. Rather, we endeavor, struggle, and even fight, not by ourselves, but through prayer, trusting in the Lord.

Question: Can outward rules and regulations like those in this training help us to develop character? These all seem to be outward. But to pray, trusting the Lord, looking to Him, seems to be more inward. Are both useful?

Answer: It is difficult to say that looking to the Lord is only inward. To look unto the Lord or to trust in the Lord is both inward and outward. We do have an attitude and we also hold such a spirit that we are looking unto Him, trusting Him to do things for us. Even this is a kind of character, a good Christian character. This is something every seeking Christian should have. All day long we should have an attitude that we are looking to the Lord, trusting in Him, and praying to Him. When we are such persons, our colleagues or co-workers who are with us daily and weekly will notice that we are people who trust in the Lord. This is our cooperation with the Lord. We are linked to Him, joined to Him, as one spirit (1 Cor. 6:17). So, we must live such a life, doing everything by trusting in Him through prayer.

THE EXPERIENCE AND GROWTH IN LIFE

MESSAGE TWENTY-NINE

THE GROWTH IN LIFE

(14)

THE PRINCIPLE OF INCARNATION FOR THE CHRISTIAN LIFE

The Christian Life Being in the Principle of Incarnation

The Christian life is a life in the principle of incarnation. Because many Christians have not seen the principle of incarnation, there have been many debates concerning the nature of the Christian life. Some have said that the Christian life is an exchanged life. This understanding of the Christian life, however, is not correct. As Christians we have a dual nature. We are no longer merely men. We are God-men. Before the incarnation of Jesus, the New Testament had not come into being. The New Testament would not be possible without the incarnation. The incarnation of Jesus initiated and ushered in the New Testament. Now we, the New Testament believers, are wonderful persons who have God in us and have been made one with God. How glorious it is to be one with God, to be a God-man.

God's Speaking in the Principle of Incarnation

In the Old Testament, when the prophets prophesied for God, their prophecies many times began with, "The word of the Lord came unto me" (Jer. 1:4; Ezek. 3:16; Isa. 38:4) or "Thus saith the Lord" (Isa. 7:7; Jer. 2:2; Ezek. 2:4). This indicates that the Lord was separate from the prophets. The word of Jehovah came objectively upon the speakers, and they declared that it was not their word but the Lord's. However, in 1 Corinthians 7:25 Paul said, "Now concerning virgins I have no commandment of the Lord, but I give my opinion as having received mercy of the Lord to be faithful;" and in giving his opinion he said, "But I think that I also have the Spirit of God" (7:40). Paul indicated that what he spoke was not a word from the Lord; it was his opinion. Yet in the giving of his opinion was the speaking of God. God lived in Paul and spoke in Paul's speaking, even in his opinion, because God had become one with Paul and had made Paul one with Him. While we are speaking, it is not only we but Christ, the embodiment of God, who speaks with us and speaks in our speaking. This is the principle of incarnation.

Hebrews 1:1-2a says, "In many portions and in many ways, God, having spoken of old to the fathers in the prophets, has at the last of these days spoken to us in the Son." On the one hand, the book of Hebrews was written anonymously. In this book the Old Testament is quoted without mentioning the names of the speakers (1:5-13; 2:6-8a; 3:7-11; 4:3-5; 8:8-12; 10:5-7, 15-17). On the other hand, Hebrews is the speaking of God in the Son. Hebrews 3:7 says, "Wherefore, even as the Holy Spirit says," and 10:15 says, "And the Holy Spirit also testifies to us." The speaker in Hebrews is not merely Paul, the Psalmist, or Jeremiah, but the Spirit.

The entire New Testament, from Matthew to Revelation, is God's speaking in the Son. In the four Gospels God spoke in the Son, and in Acts through Revelation God continued to speak in the Son. In the four Gospels He spoke through Jesus Christ, but in Acts through Revelation the outward form of His speaking changed, and He spoke in the Son through the apostles. The speaking of the apostles was the Son's speaking because the apostles had become one with the Son. Christ is the firstborn Son of God, and we are the many sons of God (Rom. 8:29; Heb. 2:10). God has many sons, and the many sons have been incorporated. The Firstborn plus the many sons are the collective, corporate Son. For this reason, God's speaking through the apostles is referred to as God's speaking in the Son.

When the Lord Jesus as the Spirit spoke through Peter, that was God speaking in the Son because Peter was one with the Son. Paul wrote more than Peter, having received the commission to complete the word of God concerning His mystery in His economy (Col. 1:25-26), but Revelation, the conclusion of the holy Word, was written by John. However, the entire New Testament is the speaking of the processed God in the person of the Son (Heb. 1:2). Moreover, the Son is not the Son alone, but the Son with all His members. We are the members of the Body of Christ, and the Body is composed of all the sons of God. God begot many children to become His sons, and these sons are the components of the Body of Christ. Therefore, we are the members of the Son. Today God is still speaking in the corporate Son in the principle of incarnation.

THE CHRISTIAN LIFE AS A LIFE
WITH THE PROCESSED AND DISPENSING GOD

The Christian life is a life in which God's chosen, redeemed, regenerated, and saved people live together with the processed and dispensing God. The Christian life is something particular. Not everybody can live such a life. Only we who have been chosen, redeemed, and saved by God can live together with the processed and dispensing God. This is a life in the principle of incarnation, and it is a mingled life, a life in which God and man are mingled together.

In whatever we do, we have to realize that we are persons mingled with the processed and dispensing God. We are not alone. When we are exchanging words with our spouse, we must realize that God is within us. This will stop the exchange of words. When we are going to a certain place, we must remember that we are persons mingled with God and that God is going with us. When we are reminded that we are mingled with Him, it seems that it is we who are remembering. However, our remembering at this time does not actually come from us. It comes from Christ as our Partner, who is one with us. When an unbeliever goes to a movie theater, he does not have the thought that God is going with him because he does not have Christ as his Partner. However, wherever we go, we have a Partner.

We are particular, peculiar persons. Wherever we are, we are not alone. Another One is with us all the time. Many

Christians can testify of their experience of God in this way. Certain persons used to gamble before they were saved, but after being saved, they were no longer able to gamble. As an unbeliever I spent much time playing soccer. After I was saved, I continued to play soccer because I felt it was not sinful. However, one day when the ball came to me on the soccer field, I felt as if I could not use my foot to kick it. I turned and walked off the field. From that time on I never went back to play soccer. Even at that time I did not consciously realize that I was not alone and that the Lord Jesus was with me. I thought it was I alone who was walking off the field. Many Christians have had a similar experience. We did not realize that it was not merely we who acted, but the processed and dispensing God, who is Christ consummated as the Spirit.

The Christian life is a life that we, the God-chosen, redeemed, and saved people, live together with the processed and dispensing God, a life lived by two persons mingled together and living together as one. Whether or not we intend to live such a life, as long as we are Christians, especially seeking Christians, we are living with Christ as the all-inclusive embodiment of the Triune God, the Father, the Son, and the life-giving Spirit. Even if we would repent of being Christians, it is too late. Something has gotten into us, and we can never be rid of it. The Lord's recovery is to recover such a life, that the God-chosen, redeemed, regenerated, and saved people may live together, consciously or unconsciously, intentionally or unintentionally, with the processed and dispensing God. When we live such a life, we declare that we are chosen, redeemed, regenerated, and saved. We are not persons of ourselves. We are persons of the choosing, redeeming, regenerating, and saving God. We declare that the processed and dispensing God lives with us. Not only do we live with Him, but He lives with us.

Before we were saved, we may have rarely asked ourselves if what we were doing was proper. We may have thought that everything we did was right. Today, however, the Lord often interrupts us and questions us about what we are doing. We may think that we are asking ourselves this question. However, we must realize that it is not merely we, but our Partner who is asking it. Our Partner is one with us and sometimes appears to be us. Galatians 2:20 says, "I have been crucified with Christ, and it is no longer I who live, but Christ lives in me; and the life which I now live in the flesh I live in faith, the faith of the Son of God, who loved me and gave Himself for me." In the first part of this verse, the "I" is the old man; in the second part, the "I" is a new person who is one with Christ as his Partner.

There is always One within us who reminds us that we are one with Him. Before I was saved, I could do things without limitation. Now, however, I am a different person. Sometimes when I have laughed too much, my Partner questioned whether my laughter was of the Spirit, and my laughter stopped. Before I was saved, when I lost my temper, I lost it without constraint. However, after I was saved, I experienced that while I was losing my temper, there was something within me restraining me. Experiences such as these prove we are saved. God is here, not only with us, but one with us. He lives with us in our living, and He is waiting for our cooperation, that our living would be one with His.

In John 14:19 Jesus said, "Because I live, you shall live also." Apparently, the Lord lives by Himself and we live by ourselves. However, John 14:16-20 tells us that we live together. When He lives, we live in His living, and when we live, He lives in our living. This is a deep mystery. Apparently, John 14:19 is a simple word, but its significance is very deep. The very God lives together with man, the sinful and dirtied man who has been chosen, redeemed, regenerated, and saved. This is the Christian life.

Hallelujah, we were chosen, redeemed, regenerated, and saved. We did not choose Him. Rather, we may have rejected Him. We cannot explain what happened to cause us to believe in the Lord. It was not up to us. We simply changed our mind and called on His name. Now we are persons who are mingled with the Lord. When we go along with Him, we are happy. When we do not go along with Him, we have no rest. Christians are not always a people of rest. Many times we are bothered by something within. We may even spend more time being troubled than resting. The One who troubles us is our Partner. Because of our Partner, we are here in the church and have dropped many things to concentrate ourselves on the Christian life.

If we realize what the Christian life is, we are truly blessed. We are one with Him. This is our rest and our testimony. Unconsciously and spontaneously, we are living a life with God. When we live, He lives. When we speak, He speaks. Wherever we go, He goes also. We cannot deny this reality, and we cannot reject it. This is the Christian life. The Christian life does not need our strife and struggle to do good. Struggling in this way can produce results only for a short time. We simply should live a life with God. Paul said, "For to me to live is Christ" (Phil. 1:21). In his living, he was one with Christ, living Christ and expressing Christ. Eventually, it will be no longer we who live, but Christ who lives in us.

THE EXPERIENCE AND GROWTH IN LIFE

MESSAGE THIRTY

THE EXPERIENCE OF LIFE

(16)

In this message I will give a further conclusion to the fellowship concerning the experience of life. This conclusion has two parts that we should remember. The first part is to remember that we now have Christ within us as our Partner all the time. We no longer live, behave, act, and have our being by ourselves. We must remember that the Lord is living within us. The second part is that we must remember what kind of person we are.

REMEMBERING THAT THE LORD IS WITHIN US

The Christian life is a life of man being mingled with God. It is a life of two persons being mingled together and living together. It is not a matter of living a life by yourself. As a Christian you must always keep in mind that you are no longer by yourself. Another One is always with you as a Partner, both in the small things and in the big things. The unbelievers do not have such a One with them in their experience; therefore, they do not understand this kind of language. As you are in your daily activities, you should realize that another invisible One is with you and indwelling you.

Sometimes, we do not like the fact that He is dwelling within us because we are not able to do or say things so freely. When we are about to lose our temper, we have to consider Him. We must consider whether or not He likes to lose the temper with us. We have another One living within us, so we must live a life which never neglects, forgets, or disregards Him.

We must learn to always live a life with another Person inside of us. This should always be our spontaneous experience, but today it is still only our occasional experience. Without remembering that the Lord is within us, we may be free to like or dislike anyone according to our own choice. But when we remember that He is with us, our freedom is greatly reduced. Marriage reduces our freedom because we have to learn to live with another person. Before a brother marries, he is free to exercise his own likes or dislikes and to go wherever he likes. But after he is married, he always has another one with him. Quite often, the husband is frustrated from doing what he likes by his wife, and the wife is also frustrated by the husband. The husband may want to laugh, but because of his wife, he may not be free to do so. Before marriage, he had no such restrictions or frustrations, but after marriage, he has a lot of restrictions. Having a wife or husband really restricts our freedom, but our wife or husband can also be a great benefit to us, especially in the way of companionship.

From my youth, I have sought to know how to live the Christian life, how to be holy, and how to be victorious. I have read many Christian publications on this subject. Eventually, I found out that not one of the ways presented in these books was really prevailing. According to my own experience, only the way of remembering that He is within us really works. The problem we have is that we often forget that He is within us. During our daily life, we just do not remember that the Lord as another One is with us. But when we do remember and realize that He is within us, everything is okay.

REMEMBERING WHAT KIND OF PEOPLE WE ARE

In our practical Christian experience, we must always remember what we are. We must remember that according to our fallen nature, we are corrupt and evil. When we appreciate or think very highly of ourselves, we can easily be mistaken. When spouses lose their temper and exchange words with one another, if the husband considers himself to be better than his wife, his anger seems to increase. But if the husband remembers that he is mean, dirty, ugly, and altogether of no use, his anger will be reduced. Sometimes, as we are about to criticize someone else, we are reminded about our own condition. This kind of remembrance always keeps us in our proper place and saves us from making mistakes. Every day we all need to be reminded concerning what kind of people we are.

We were created by God in a wonderful way, but we were also spoiled and contaminated by Satan. We were redeemed and saved by the Lord, but we still have our fallen body which is full of filthy, evil lusts. For this reason we groan that we might be delivered from our corrupted, fallen body (Rom. 8:23). Because our entire being was contaminated, we need the blood of Jesus Christ to continually and constantly cleanse us from all sin (1 John 1:7). The cleansing of the blood is like a shower which runs all the time. Under this cleansing current, contamination is taken away. But when we are not under this cleansing, contamination returns. Therefore, we need to apply the cleansing of the blood many times throughout the day.

In the Old Testament, the priests offered many offerings daily. These offerings signify Christ in His various aspects. We must offer Christ as our daily sin offering and trespass offering for our continual cleansing (see *Experiencing Christ as the Offerings for the Church Meetings,* pp. 69-97, published by the Living Stream Ministry). Many times throughout the day we need to apply the blood of Christ to our case.

The remembrance of our rottenness and corruption saves, safeguards, and protects us. To consider that we are above others because of our level of education or national heritage really damages us. We must always realize and be reminded that we are corrupt people, that our body of flesh is full of lusts, that our soul is saturated with the evil one, making our self the embodiment of Satan (Matt. 16:23), and that our spirit is deadened. Though our spirit has certainly been regenerated (John 3:6), it is still under a deadening condition today. Second Corinthians 7:1 says that we must cleanse ourselves from all defilement of flesh and spirit. This defilement of our spirit is the deadening of our spirit. The reason our spirit is often empty, dry, low, and contaminated is because it is not so living. Because our spirit is deadened, it is easy for us to lose our temper or to criticize others, but it is difficult to praise the Lord. At morning watch, our spirit may become very living, but at other times during the day, our spirit is not so living. So, it is easy for it to be contaminated. A lifeless, wooden pole can easily become dirty or contaminated, but not a living tree.

HAVING NO CONFIDENCE IN THE FLESH

When we remember that we are persons whose bodies are full of lust, whose souls have become one with Satan, and whose spirits are deadened, we will have no confidence or trust in ourselves. Paul was such a person. According to Philippians 3:3, Paul boasted in Christ Jesus and had no confidence in the flesh. He had no confidence in himself, so he did not trust in himself. This kind of experience brought Paul to trust in the Lord Himself. We need to experience the same thing. We must realize that there is no one for us to trust in but Christ. Our trust must altogether be in Him, and without Him, we are just pitiful people. We should not say that we are anything; it is better for us to say that we are nothing. We are pitiful people who need the Lord.

In order to know the experience and growth of life, we do need to know a number of different teachings throughout the Bible. Yet, in addition to these things, we also need to know two very crucial things. First, we need to know that the Lord Jesus has made Himself one with us (1 Cor. 6:17). As a result, we should no longer live a life by ourselves; we must live a life with Him. Second, we must know that our entire being—spirit, soul, and body—has been corrupted. Therefore, we should have no trust or confidence in ourselves. With these two realizations, we may pray, "Lord, I have no trust or confidence in myself. My trust is altogether in You. Without You, I am just a pitiful person. Without You or apart from You, I can do nothing. But in You, the One who empowers me, I can do all things." This is the Christian life.

PETER'S EXPERIENCE OF KNOWING HIMSELF

Before the Lord's crucifixion Peter was very confident in himself that he would not deny the Lord (Matt. 26:33-35). So, the Lord in His sovereignty arranged the environment for Peter to deny Him three times, even in front of the Lord's face (Luke 22:55-61). Through those kinds of experiences, Peter was subdued. After the Lord's resurrection according to John 21, the Lord met Peter at a place where he and the other disciples were backsliding (v. 1). As they were fishing, the Lord appeared on the seashore. When they saw the Lord, they realized that they were naked (v. 7). This is very meaningful. The Lord met Peter in a backslidden condition when he had no covering.

When they arrived on the seashore and while they ate breakfast, Peter was very subdued and was probably not very comfortable. He may have felt very ashamed because of his recent failures: he had denied the Lord, he had not remained in Jerusalem, the place where the Lord had charged him to stay (Luke 24:49), and he had taken the lead to backslide, going back to Galilee to pick up his old job of fishing (John 21:3). Peter might have been excited to see the Lord inwardly, but due to his failures, he may not have had the faith to express his feeling outwardly.

After breakfast, the Lord asked Peter a question, "Simon, son of John, do you love Me more than these?" Peter responded to the Lord by saying, "Yes, Lord, You know that I love You." Peter's response indicates a great deal. He did not just say, "Yes, Lord, I love You" nor did he say, "No, Lord, I'm sorry. I'd like to love You, but I cannot love You." Peter's answer to the Lord's question reveals that he was really subdued. He had lost all confidence in himself. Peter's confidence had been transferred from himself to the Lord. Because he no longer had any confidence in himself, he wanted to know what the Lord would say. He may have remembered both his own confident declaration that he would never deny the Lord and the Lord's word that he would deny Him three times. Through this failure Peter realized that only what the Lord said really counted. So, when the Lord questioned Peter, Peter turned the question back to the Lord to see what He would say. By this little word, you can see that Peter, having no confidence in himself, was subdued and broken. This is the Christian life, a life which is subdued and broken.

A SPECIAL WORD TO THE TRAINEES
CONCERNING GOING BACK TO VISIT
THEIR SUPPORTING CHURCHES

As trainees, you may have become disappointed or discouraged by your experience of exposure in this training. Because of this, you may consider to withdraw from the training to go back to the church which supported you. Your going back in this way may make you even more miserable. Because you do not know yourself, you may think that you need to do something. Actually, you do not need to do anything. You simply need to tell the Lord, "Lord, here I am. I am pitiful. I have no confidence in myself. My confidence and trust is just in You. Without You or apart from You, I am just a pitiful person." To come to this realization is really positive.

Your attitude in visiting your supporting church, parents, and relatives is very important. If you go back with an attitude and realization that you are nothing and that your confidence is really in the Lord, this would be wonderful. Such a testimony would nourish everyone who listens to you. But if you go back testifying how marvelous the training was, everyone who hears your testimony may be killed. If your experience with the Lord in the training was proper, you were being exposed every day. Everything in the training only served to expose you. Such experiences are very profitable, because it indicates that you are beginning to really know yourself. Though you have learned and been equipped with a great deal in this training, this learning may be considered as only some "gold" to adorn you outwardly. To give people the impression that you are now gilded with gold would not be so fitting. The best impression to give others is that you are a broken and subdued person with no apparent gold. If your supporting church would receive such an impression from you, this would be very profitable.

THE EXPERIENCE AND GROWTH IN LIFE

MESSAGE THIRTY-ONE

THE GROWTH IN LIFE

(15)

In the previous chapters we have seen that the Christian life is a mingling of two persons living together as one. We have also seen who we are. We are flesh, and our spirit was deadened and our soul contaminated. As such we have no confidence in our self. In this chapter, we will see who Christ is. If we are seeking after the growth in the divine life and seeking to live the Christian life, we should always remember who our Savior is. We have not exhausted the knowledge of Christ. The knowledge of Christ that many Christians have is too limited, shallow, traditional, and even superstitious. Many hold an inadequate concept of Christ in the divine Trinity and do not realize how Christ's person is related to God's economy.

CHRIST AS THE DIVINE SPIRIT BEING MINGLED WITH OUR HUMAN SPIRIT

Christ our Savior is God (Rom. 9:5; Heb. 1:8), the Son (Matt. 16:16), and the Spirit (1 Cor. 15:45b). In total, He is the processed and dispensing Triune God who is consummated as the Spirit. The Spirit of God is the consummated Spirit, the consummation of the processed Triune God. The writings of John reveal much concerning the divine Spirit and our human spirit. John 3:2-13 is a portion of the Word on regeneration. In this chapter the term *Holy Spirit* is not used. Verses 5, 6, and 8 simply refer to "the Spirit." John 7:39 also speaks of the Spirit, saying, "But this He said concerning the Spirit, whom those who believed in Him were about to receive; for the Spirit was not yet, because Jesus was not yet glorified." Finally, Revelation 22:17 says, "And the Spirit and the bride say, Come."

John 3:6 and 4:24 speak of the two spirits, the divine Spirit and the human spirit. John 3:6 says, "That which is born of the flesh is flesh, and that which is born of the Spirit is spirit." John 4:24 says, "God is Spirit; and those who worship Him must worship in spirit and reality." The divine Spirit begets our human spirit, and our human spirit worships the divine Spirit. As a result, our human spirit is filled with the divine Spirit.

Paul also speaks much concerning the divine Spirit and our human spirit in the Epistles. Many times Paul's references to the Spirit are difficult to translate because Paul often used the word *spirit* to denote the mingled spirit. Many references to the spirit in the Epistles actually denote the divine Spirit mingled with the human spirit. The mingled spirit is indicated several times in Galatians 5. Verses 16 and 17 say, "But I say, walk by the Spirit and you shall by no means fulfill the lust of the flesh. For the flesh lusts against the Spirit, and the Spirit against the flesh." Verse 25 says, "If we live by the Spirit, let us also walk by the Spirit." The Spirit in these verses, according to the context of the chapter, is the Holy Spirit, who dwells in and mingles with our regenerated spirit. To walk by the Spirit is to have our walk regulated by the Holy Spirit from within our spirit. In verse 17 it is the mingled spirit, the divine Spirit with our human spirit, that is contrary to the flesh.

In Romans 8:16 Paul says, "The Spirit Himself witnesses with our spirit that we are the children of God." In this verse the two spirits are no longer separate. The divine Spirit is with our human spirit, and the two spirits have become the mingled spirit.

CHRIST AS THE PROCESSED
AND CONSUMMATED TRIUNE GOD

Our Savior is Jesus Christ, the Son of God. The Son is the embodiment of the Father, and the Spirit is the realization of the Son. After the Triune God passed through all His processes, the Spirit became the consummated Spirit, the consummation of the Triune God. In eternity past God was perfect. He was the divine Person, almighty, unlimited, and eternal. However, in eternity past He did not possess the human nature since He had not yet been born of a human virgin. He had not passed through human life for thirty-three and a half years. He also had not yet entered into death and walked through it, and He did not yet have the experience of resurrection. He was in the heavens, but He had not yet descended from the heavens to the earth, descended further to Hades, risen up from the realm of death and darkness, and entered into resurrection. He had not ascended to the heavens, not only in His divinity, but also in His incarnation, His human living, all-inclusive death, and all-empowering resurrection. Today, however, after passing through all these processes, He is the consummated Triune God. He is not only perfect but also completed.

CHRIST BEING ONE WITH HIS MEMBERS

As believers in Christ we have been made one with God and have become the members of Christ. God is embodied in Christ, and Christ is both the individual Christ and the corporate Christ. The individual Christ is simply Christ Himself, but the corporate Christ is Christ with all His members. God has made Himself one with man and has made man one with Him. The oneness of Christ with His members is seen in Acts 9. In Acts 9:4 the Lord Jesus said to Paul, "Saul, Saul, why are you persecuting Me?" Paul had never persecuted the individual Jesus. He persecuted the members of Christ, yet Christ considered that as a persecution against Himself. In Philippians 1:21 Paul said, "For to me to live is Christ." This indicates Paul's oneness with Christ. First Corinthians 6:17 also shows that we and Christ are one wonderful entity. This verse says, "But he who is joined to the Lord is one spirit." The one spirit in this verse is the mingled spirit.

The early church fathers in their writings used the word *mingling* to describe our oneness with the Lord. They also taught that the believers were "deified" by being joined to the Lord. However, in using these terms there is the possibility of being misunderstood. When we say that we are one with God, we do not mean that we become the person of God. This is to make ourselves an object of worship and should be condemned as blasphemy. To be one with God is to be one with Him in His divine life and nature. Every life produces offspring after its own kind (Gen. 1:11, 21, 24). As children of our physical father we have our father's life and nature, but we are not the same person as he is. A grandfather, a father, and a son all have the same life and nature, but they are different persons. In life and nature they are the same, but in person they are different. As the children of God (Rom. 8:16; 1 John 3:1) we have been "deified," not in person but in life and in nature. We are one with God in His life and nature, but not in His person.

CHRIST AS THE GOD-MAN
IN DEATH AND RESURRECTION

Christ is a God-man, a man born of two natures, the divine nature and the human nature. He lived a human life on the earth and passed through trials and temptations. As the God-man He also entered into death and accomplished an all-inclusive death. Christ's death terminated everything negative in the universe. His all-inclusive death ended sin, Satan, the flesh, the old creation, our old man, and everything negative. Then He was buried with all the items which He had terminated through His death. Our old man was buried with Christ (Rom. 6:4, 6). Sin, sins, and the devil were also buried in Christ's tomb. Many times Satan attacks us under different cloaks. To Eve he came in the cloak of a serpent. Many times he comes to us in the cloak of a person or a situation to tempt us. At that time we should tell him not to remain with us, but to return to the tomb. Christ came out of the tomb in resurrection, and in resurrection He ascended to the heavens.

CHRIST AS THE REALITY OF
ALL POSITIVE THINGS

As we have seen, Christ is the Triune God—the Father, the Son, and the Spirit—and He is the embodiment of God. Christ is many other items, such as the reality of the plants

mentioned positively in the Bible. Christ is the real cedar tree
(Lev. 14:4; 1 Kings 6:9), the real hyssop (Lev. 14:4; Psa. 51:7),
and the real henna flower (S. S. 1:14, ASV). The chorus of
#171 in *Hymns* says,

> Lord, like the pretty henna-flower,
> In vineyards blossoming Thou art;
> Incomp'rable Thy beauty is,
> Admires and loves our heart!

At the time the Song of Solomon was written, the henna
flower was used by women as a cosmetic. We should take
Christ as our beauty. Christ is also the apple tree (S. S. 2:3).
The word translated "apple" in Song of Solomon 2:3 is actually the word for a juicy and nourishing tropical fruit. We
need to be beautified with Christ as the henna flower and
nourished with Christ as the fruit. Moreover, we can sit under His shadow to rest, enjoy, and relax (S. S. 2:3). Christ is
also the plant of renown in Ezekiel 34:29.

Christ is the reality of everything positive. Colossians
2:16-17 says, "Let no one therefore judge you in eating and
in drinking or in respect of a feast or of a new moon or Sab-
baths, which are a shadow of things to come, but the body is
of Christ." Christ is the reality of the Sabbath and the festi-
vals in the Old Testament. Christ is also our food (John
6:32-35), our drink (John 4:10-14), and our real joy. He is
the air, the breath, the soil, and our good land. This is our
Savior.

We need to remember Him as all these things. Every week
we have at least one meeting for the purpose of coming
together to remember Him. At the Lord's Table we display His
death for the remembrance of Him. We need to improve our
praises at the Lord's Table meeting. We should pray, "Lord,
You are our henna flower for our beauty, and You are the fruit
for our nourishment." If we do not praise Him in this way, it
indicates that we do not have the proper knowledge of Christ
from the Bible. If we have the adequate knowledge of Christ,
we will praise Him adequately at His table.

Because Christ is so many positive items, the church also
becomes many items. Verse 4 of Hymn #203 says,

> We're Thy total reproduction,
>   Thy dear Body and Thy Bride,
> Thine expression and Thy fulness,
>   For Thee ever to abide.
> We are Thy continuation,
>   Thy life-increase and Thy spread,
> Thy full growth and Thy rich surplus,
>   One with Thee, our glorious Head.

The church is all these items because Christ is so much.

We must remember what the Christian life is, who we are, and who Christ is. Then day after day we will be refreshed and revived. We will be overcoming and victorious, and we will spread Him. We will bear the responsibility to dispense Him to others, not only to sinners, but also to weaker, younger Christians.

ABOUT THE AUTHOR

Witness Lee was born in 1905 in northern China and raised in a Christian family. At age 19 he was fully captured for Christ and immediately consecrated himself to preach the gospel for the rest of his life. Early in his service, he met Watchman Nee, a renowned preacher, teacher, and writer. Witness Lee labored together with Watchman Nee under his direction. In 1934 Watchman Nee entrusted Witness Lee with the responsibility for his publication operation, called the Shanghai Gospel Bookroom.

Prior to the Communist takeover in 1949, Witness Lee was sent by Watchman Nee and his other co-workers to Taiwan to ensure that the things delivered to them by the Lord would not be lost. Watchman Nee instructed Witness Lee to continue the former's publishing operation abroad as the Taiwan Gospel Bookroom, which has been publicly recognized as the publisher of Watchman Nee's works outside China. Witness Lee's work in Taiwan manifested the Lord's abundant blessing. From a mere 350 believers, newly fled from the mainland, the churches in Taiwan grew to 20,000 in five years.

In 1962 Witness Lee felt led of the Lord to come to the United States, settling in California. During his 35 years of service in the U.S., he ministered in weekly meetings and weekend conferences, delivering several thousand spoken messages. Much of his speaking has since been published as over 400 titles. Many of these have been translated into over fourteen languages. He gave his last public conference in February 1997 at the age of 91.

He leaves behind a prolific presentation of the truth in the Bible. His major work, *Life-study of the Bible,* comprises over 25,000 pages of commentary on every book of the Bible from the perspective of the believers' enjoyment and experience of God's divine life in Christ through the Holy Spirit. Witness Lee was the chief editor of a new translation of the New Testament into Chinese called the Recovery Version and directed the translation of the same into English. The Recovery Version also appears in a number of other languages. He provided an extensive body of footnotes, outlines, and spiritual cross references. A radio broadcast of his messages can be heard on Christian radio stations in the United States. In 1965 Witness Lee founded Living Stream Ministry, a non-profit corporation, located in Anaheim, California, which officially presents his and Watchman Nee's ministry.

Witness Lee's ministry emphasizes the experience of Christ as life and the practical oneness of the believers as the Body of Christ. Stressing the importance of attending to both these matters, he led the churches under his care to grow in Christian life and function. He was unbending in his conviction that God's goal is not narrow sectarianism but the Body of Christ. In time, believers began to meet simply as the church in their localities in response to this conviction. In recent years a number of new churches have been raised up in Russia and in many eastern European countries.